FOREWORD BY

Author, The Courageous Follower: Sta

THE LEADERSHIP MYTH

Why Leadership Principles Do Not Work In Sub-Saharan Africa

TOYE SOBANDE

Published by **Toye Sobande**
Stephens Leadership Consultancy LLC
110, W Randol Mill Rd,
Suite 240 Arlington, TX 76011,
United States

ISBN 978-1-9196022-0-2

Cover Concept & Layout Design
Phoster Solutions, Lagos, Nigeria.
www.phosterng.com

Praise Reports

Arguably one of the most contemporary, realistic, and incisive books on why acclaimed leadership principles do not always work in Africa. Sobande writes with amazing clarity and logic, providing lucid explanations to sometimes complex concepts and in it he is both enlightening and persuasive. A brilliant and timely intervention. -
–**Frank Aigbogun, Publisher and Editor-In-Chief of BusinessDay Media Limited**

This book challenges African leaders in all sectors and industries to embrace her emblematic rich heritage, as demonstrated by her past great leaders during the pre-colonial era. Who modelled a leadership ideology centred on African values and belief system established on trustworthiness, honour, mutual respect, collaboration, creativity, and hard work. To date, Africa has produced some of the finest and brightest global leaders against the ill narrative by the media agencies of its detractors who belittles the continent in other to continue to exploit her mineral and human resources. Toye Sobande opined that Africa's liberation and development are realizable if Africans can be more Afrocentric. This book is a must-read for all.
- **Richard Mofe-Damijo, Actor, Lawyer, PR Expert and Former Commissioner of Information and Culture, Delta State.**

This book has a very big heart. It also tackles a very big subject. Sobande painstakingly creates distinctions between Western managerialism and African communalism. His book is rich with what is needed to revive the latter to the benefit of the governed. Implicit in the values and mechanisms of traditional African culture is the dialogue between followers and their formal leaders. When done well and with the right intention, this elevates the character and practice of leadership. There may be some romanticizing of traditional culture. Nevertheless, focusing on its normative qualities provides a potential Southern Cross for guiding African followership and leadership.

- **Ira Chaleff, Author: The Courageous Follower: Standing Up to and For Our Leaders**

Finally, I have found a book, a well-written body of work, opening my eyes to why Western leadership theories are not efficient in Africa and how a return to Africa's pre-colonial leadership values may hold the key to our renaissance. Instructive and illuminating.

– **Simon Kolawole, Publisher and Chief Executive Officer of Cable Newspaper Limited**

Dedication

To my loving Father
Stephen Olanrewaju Sobande
A man of honour, who illuminated the path for me and my
siblings and taught me about Leadership, Love, and Faith

Acknowledgement

I am indebted to the many authors and thinkers on whose work I have relied on over the years. This book would not have been possible without them, but I also feel incredibly honoured that readers might credit me for the insights that originated from other, wiser writers. I am privileged to be a beneficiary of their valuable contributions to humanity.

This book would not be what it is without the editing and valuable advice of my editors, Emmanuel Egbo, Blessing James and Tharanga Gamage, who provided critical notes early on that I am very grateful for. I appreciate Dr Bola Oyelakin-Ogungbadejo for her kindness and support in bringing this book to reality.

To my lovely mother, Lady Abigail Oladunni Sobande JP, my sisters, Cecilia Olayinka Odimayomi, Elizabeth Ola-oluwa Obajolu, and my brothers, Dr Patrick Olamidotun Sobande and Engr. Christopher Oladipupo Sobande who are excellent role models in how to live and appreciate life. I thank them for their guidance and conversations with me about their leadership journey.

Also, I owe a debt of gratitude to my lovely wife, Princess Ediri Sobande, famously known as "Awelewa," whose exceptional love, patience, encouragement, and support made this book possible. I want to thank my Children, Jemimah and Alexander Sobande, for being my greatest cheerleaders. Your global perspectives fascinate me every time I listen to both of you.

And for my education and life experiences, I thank my friends, colleagues, teachers, and lecturers at Ikeja Grammar School, Lagos State Polytechnic (LASPOTECH), Obafemi Awolowo University, Ile-Ife; University of Buckingham, United Kingdom; Regent University, USA, for instilling in me the virtue of character and the spirit of scholarship, which facilitated the writing of this book.

I am heartily grateful to you all.

Foreword by Ira Chaleff

This book has a very big heart. It also tackles a very big subject. Centuries of colonialism overwhelmed traditional African cultures and forms of communal governance.

As African countries achieved independence, the values of colonial overlords often remained entrenched. The history of post-colonial African governance has borne the marks of leadership that insufficiently reflects traditional African values.

Sobande painstakingly creates distinctions between Western managerialism and African communalism. His book is rich with what is needed to revive the latter to the benefit of the governed. Implicit in the values and mechanisms of traditional African culture is the dialogue between followers and their formal leaders. When done well and with the right intention, this elevates the character and practice of leadership.

There may be some romanticizing of traditional culture. Nevertheless, focusing on its normative qualities provides a potential Southern Cross for guiding current and future African followership and leadership.

—Ira Chaleff,
Author: The Courageous Follower: Standing Up To and For Our Leaders

Table of Contents

Introduction

Africans have this thing called UBUNTU. It is about the essence of being human; it is part of the gift that Africa will give the world. It embraces hospitality, caring about others, being able to go the extra mile for the sake of others. We believe that a person is a person through another person, that my humanity is caught up, bound up, inextricably, with yours

– Desmond Tutu, Emeritus Archbishop of Cape Town.

Figure 1: Geographical map of sub-Saharan Africa

Sub-Saharan Africa - what does the name bring to mind? For some, it evokes painful memories of anguish, poverty, and war. For some, it is synonymous with warm and friendly people. For some, it depicts a region ruled by dictators and tyrants. Yet, for others, it conjures up images of a resource-rich continent but largely an agglomeration of poor countries. All these form part of the bigger picture of Sub-Saharan Africa.

Some years ago, any enquiry outside of Sub-Saharan Africa would probably have discovered that the words most commonly associated with the region were "war," "military coup," "disease," "poverty," and the like – that is words with negative connotations. The 46 countries of Sub-Saharan Africa were often referred to as "Black Africa," and the whole continent labelled the "Dark Continent" with racist connotations. Today, this is no longer the case. The new labels for Africa are "open for business," "African solutions for Africa," "emerging market," etc. It must be noted that this optimism is borne by the emergence of a new breed of leaders who seem to believe that African problems can only be effectively tackled by Africans themselves.

This is the primary reason for writing this book. This book provides a research-based, pragmatic understanding of African leadership principles and what is effective in Sub-Saharan Africa. Sub-Saharan Africa is a vast geographical area with 46 countries and hundreds of cultures. Therefore, in this book, I have tried to paint a broad picture of the region and provide a detailed expose of the leadership myth therein. The book emerged from my research, travels, and interactions with people within the geopolitical zone. The studies have been reviewed and restructured to conform to the topic – **The Leadership Myth: Why Leadership Principles Do Not Work in Sub-Saharan Africa (SSA).**

This book takes a narrative approach and empirical data gathered from existing research conducted by scholars in the field, international organizations, and relevant government agencies.

Indeed, the research embraces African wisdom, acknowledging the strengths and weaknesses, and adopts a discursive approach. In a nutshell, it is aimed at unearthing insights from practice for practice.

The insights contained therein will be valuable for African leaders and African managers interfacing with their non-African counterparts, as well as for international organizations operating in the region such as the African Development Bank (ADB), the African Union (AU), the International Monetary Fund (IMF) and so on. A primary audience for the book is scholars in the business and economic sectors. A secondary audience is managers, both African managers and those from other countries who have a significant stake in SSA.

The chapters draw on extant research on Sub-Saharan African countries, which is used to provide a context for and a picture of the leadership myth in the region. The book succinctly brings to the fore the role of culture and its impact on leadership. It begins by examining the African experience in political leadership and how this has affected the region's socio-political development. The next chapter debunks foreign misconceptions about leadership in Sub-Saharan Africa with copious references and documented evidence. The rest chapters comprise leadership studies in the region, including historical perspectives, current realities, recommendations, and advice.

This book fills an important gap in the literature on leadership studies in Africa. Most of the existing literature focusing on leadership in SSA is based on Western perspectives, which does not adequately explain why globally tested leadership principles do not work in the region. The book's author is domiciled in Africa, and, in many ways, he provides an "insider's view" of SSA. Throughout the book, I intend to identify leadership styles across the region and compare them with leadership principles from other regions of the world. I use the comparison to highlight and explain leadership practices that are most likely effective in the African context. Thus, the book considers leadership from an Afrocentric perspective and attempts to provide answers to such pertinent questions as:

1.   What are the components of leadership from an African perspective?

2.   How does culture impact leadership in Africa?

3.   What are the similarities and differences between leadership in Africa and the Western world?

4.   Why do leadership theories fail to work in Sub-Saharan Africa?

5.   Are there reasons for Africans to look inwards for effective leadership styles?

6.   How can Sub-Saharan Africa fly to self-sufficiency with its indigenous leadership theories?

The book draws on global leadership research that includes Sub-Saharan African countries, such as the GLOBE leadership work and Hofstede's cultural value dimensions. It also draws on indigenous leadership studies, including Maat and Ubuntu. These research-based writings will ensure that the material provided in the book is evidence-based and relevant. The material will be presented in a way that will make for easy comprehension for managers, politicians, legal practitioners, scholars, students, and ordinary citizens.

This book includes anecdotal materials from academics, managers, leaders, and organizations within SSA and those connected with the region. Empirical research combined with personal experiences gives a well-rounded sense of the reality of leadership styles in the zone. One feature of the book is an attempt to unearth issues and trends in African leadership, which often tie the people's cultural values and preferences to their leadership ethos.

Although the book's title is **The Leadership Myth: Why Leadership Principles Do Not Work in Sub-Saharan Africa,** I acknowledge that it is impossible to cover all countries in the region. Sub-Saharan Africa is a large region with many countries and diverse cultures; only a subset is covered in this book. The discussions are broadly centred on sub-regions of East Africa, South Africa, and West Africa, especially countries with extant research. I do not attempt to cover countries where there is no existing leadership research.

1

POLITICAL LEADERSHIP: THE AFRICAN EXPERIENCE

Chapter 1

The future lies with those wise political leaders who realize that the great public is interested more in governance than in politics

– Franklin D. Roosevelt

Sub-Saharan Africa presents a unique context of study for leadership scholars. A vast expanse of landmass encompassing more than 46 countries, territories, and states with over 1 billion people. The region lies to the south of the great Sahara Desert, and its diversity of cultures, ethnicities, and languages are sources of both richness and conflict.

It is easy to experience a sense of déjà vu when discussing political leadership in Sub-Saharan Africa. The general perception is that African leaders outside of South Africa rule failed states that have acquired ignominious tags such as "corruptocracies" and "terrorocracies." As such, perspectives on political leadership in the region vary from the criminalization of the state to the recycling of elites and the view that its political leadership dispenses patrimony and utilizes state power and resources to consolidate political power.

Since leaders play a crucial role in setting political agendas and distributing resources, we must first discuss issues about political leadership experience in the region. Hence, this chapter explores the realities of leadership related to African political leaders, including trends in leadership within the imposed context of contemporary Africa. The current state in Africa is a vestige of the old colonial system. At independence, African elites tried to change this system, but they only succeeded in entrenching their selfish interests. Together with a discussion of African political leadership, I will also address new vistas of transformational leadership in Africa as indicated by landmark initiatives like the African Union (AU), the African Peer Review Mechanism (APRM), and the New Partnership for Africa's Development (NEPAD).

An Overview of Contemporary Political Leadership in Sub-Saharan Africa

The international perception of SSA as a region dominated by inter-ethnic conflicts has primarily overshadowed the significant progress made towards stable and accountable political systems. According to a publication by the Organization for Economic Cooperation and Development (OECD), more governments in Africa are adhering to the rule of law and, by 2006, two out of every five African countries were seen as democracies. However, African politics and political institutions do not conform to the notion of the predominant institutionalized Western-type state system and a performance-based understanding of leaders and the state. This is because politics in the region is a game played beyond institutionalized confines in a Western political sense. It is often a typical extra-legal struggle for economic and political domination between the elites and the politicians. In essence, African politics is somewhat patrimonial and resembles a zero-sum game. In a patrimonial system, power is entrusted to an individual who wields it for selfish interest and personal aggrandizement, and their loyal supporters are selectively favoured. These loyal supporters or clients have to mobilize political support for their leaders or patrons.

Some of these traits, if not all, are evident in Africa's neo-patrimonial political system. For instance, power is often entrusted to a powerful individual in an arrangement based on both traditional and Western state structures, but not in an authentic conventional political sense. Moreover, politics in African countries is conducted within a close-knit circle of dependent groups. Although this type of political system can also be seen elsewhere, it is prevalent in Sub-Saharan Africa, where political power is personalized. Many politicians in this region see politics as a kind of business since political power grants them unfettered access to economic resources.

However, it is virtually impossible to deal with every aspect of political leadership in African states because of its complex nature. More so, research on the subject is scanty and scattered. Some recent studies on this subject have only focused on indigenous political leadership, traditional leadership, African elites, patrimonialism, political succession, autobiographies, and biographies of African leaders. However, these studies have shed light on current realities concerning political leadership in Africa. In the light of this, we have come to know that political systems in Sub-Saharan Africa range from the dominant one-party government (South Africa, Namibia, and Zimbabwe), one- or no-party state (Uganda 1986-2006), absolute monarchy (Swaziland) transitional government in Somalia, multi-party democracies in Ghana, Botswana, and Nigeria, as well as the half-democratic, half-authoritarian governments in Cameroon, Togo, Angola, Equatorial Guinea, etc. In all, African political leaders are now the primary controllers of political power in their respective states, unlike decades earlier. These include leaders who gained power by ballots and those who gained power by bullets. The former being elected in democratic elections, while the latter control specific areas and wield considerable power and influence.

Liberation Struggles: African Political Legacy

A typical example of political competition in Sub-Saharan Africa is the much-discussed struggle against colonialism. In recent times, struggles against colonialism have been felt in Eritrea, Namibia, and Sudan. Also, 'reform insurgencies' were launched in Ethiopia, Rwanda, and Somalia to control the government and arrest the drift towards anarchy. These liberation struggles left various legacies at the social and political levels. For example, struggle credentials determine access to power in some of these African countries, and it polarizes succeeding liberation movement-turned political parties into 'insiders' and 'outsiders,' depending on which side they belong to in the power game. Subsequently, activists and advocates for independence who turned into presidents are often reluctant to surrender power, and by extension, state ownership of natural resources, which is firmly held by the power holders of the hitherto liberation movements.

In many African countries, post-independence politics and political leadership revolved around the personality of their first president, as seen in Côte d'Ivoire under Félix Houphouët Boigny and Zimbabwe under Robert Mugabe. Similarly, post-liberation leaders in Africa enjoyed a sort of structural autonomy, which meant that they could implement the struggle's ideals without immersing themselves fully into the larger society. These leaders were able to secure their sovereignty by penetrating the community politically. To a large extent, they also enjoy ideological legitimation to implement their policies. In many cases, these leaders used to be cited as shining examples of exemplary political leadership in the continent. However, their governments held onto power when faced with political and economic crises, and exclusivist autocratic rules have emerged wherever these crises have occurred, drawing on the struggle's credentials and rhetoric. Examples of countries that have witnessed such a change of fortune include Zimbabwe, Burkina Faso, Mozambique, Malawi, and Kenya.

African Crises of Statehood

African states commonly share the imposition of imperial state structures and artificially created nation-states. Africans had little time to prepare for independence, and when it was achieved, the incoming leaders inherited mostly alien political structures. They were left with state structures coupled with coercive force and centralized political controls, including the army, police, and bureaucracy. These absurd contraptions later crystallized into establishing an alien political culture based on authoritarian patterns of governance, corruption, and ethnicity. Thus, controlling state resources, by every means, became the abiding purpose of politics.

Whenever the government cannot perform its statutory duties of providing essential services and security for its citizens, such a state is said to have failed. This performance-based, Western understanding of political stability and statehood highlights the state's responsibility to provide specific public services for which its citizens invest with legitimacy. Failure to provide these services often leads to crises in which the state loses its monopoly of force.

In simple terms, state failure refers to a situation whereby the structure of authority and political power falls apart in a state. Foreign Policy ranks six African states among the ten most vulnerable states in the world. These countries (Côte d'Ivoire, Chad, Congo DR, Somalia, Sudan, and Zimbabwe) are said to be experiencing a triple crisis of governance, which includes the inability of political leaders to manage intra and inter-state conflicts, lack of accountability, and the rule of law, and multi-level economic crises. Suppose we are to pause a bit and ponder over these issues. In that case, we will likely come to the same conclusion as the famous African political scientist, M. Mamdani, who wrote, "It is not just any state that is collapsing; it is specifically the colonial state in Africa that is collapsing." Hence, the African crises of statehood must be rightly described as crises of colonial edifices, and they are attempts by Africans themselves to redress past injustices. So, the crises in Angola, Mali, Somalia, Sudan, and the Central African Republic, must not be seen as crises of governance per se but crises of statehood.

Colonial Legacies

The scramble for Africa birthed states without any slight regard for ethnic cohesion and diversity. For instance, some ethnic groups found themselves partitioned and divided between different countries by the colonialists, as seen in the cases of such ethnic groups as:

- Yoruba (Nigeria, Togo, Benin Republic, and Sierra Leone)

- Hausa Nigeria, Benin Republic, Niger, Chad, Sudan, and Cameroon)

- Somali (Somalia, Ethiopia, Kenya, and Djibouti)

- Kongo (Congo DR, Angola, and the Republic of Congo)

This infamous transplantation of European concepts of statehood and its authority created artificial nation-states, which were once described by the foremost African scholar, Basil Davidson, as "the black man's burden as it held and subjugated ethnic groups within superficial political spaces. Thus, it is the politics of inclusion/exclusion by different ethnic groups that are responsible for many of Africa's intra or interstate wars.

It is pertinent to mention that all post-independence constitutions in Sub-Saharan Africa compromise major political actors and their vested interests. In many countries, the leaders took up a winner-take-all approach to politics; they contradicted the norms of good governance and amended the constitution to suit their fancy - accumulation of political power was the main objective.

The tide began to turn against authoritarian rulers in the 1990s when Africa witnessed its wave of democratization. Starting from that decade, Africans revolted against dictatorships and called for limited terms for their political leaders. Whereas only one African president accepted electoral defeat between 1960 and 1989, the corresponding figure rose to 15+ from 1990 to 2019. The end of the Cold War ushered in pro-democracy movements and the demand for constitutional reviews and multi-party politics across Sub-Saharan Africa.

It is no coincidence that the removal of the Cold War straitjacket heralded pro-democracy movements in Africa. This only reinforces the notion that Africans can redesign their institutions of governance themselves if given a chance, devoid of the overbearing influence of European and Asian countries. Those who think otherwise should take cognizance of the case of Somalia. Since it fell apart in 1991 when ethnic militias removed Siad Barre from office, the Somalis have seen no less than fourteen attempts by foreign powers to restore law and order to no avail. The efforts were simply too little and inadequate.

Besides, the Western notion of statehood does not apply to African countries. Take Ethiopia, for example; it has experimented with various political systems in the last 140 years to emulate and copy Asian and European models of governance. These alternatives include Imperial Japan and Russia, the post-WWII United Kingdom, and even a reformed Marxist model. Needless to say, their citizens were left disappointed in the course of these experiments.

African Cases of Stayism

Self-centred politics by leadership, personality politics, and personal politics are the unique features of contemporary politics in Africa. These refer to the over-centralization of political power in the executive, which leads to the institutionalization of executive political leadership in African countries. In Nigeria, for example, this phenomenon is seen in the domination of the political arena by powerful godfathers at the apogee of a vast political network at local, state, and federal levels. Hence, political contests became a fierce competition between these powerful entities, often detrimental to the larger society. Professor Ali Mazrui puts this succinctly when he described the African political system as patriarchal – this is a situation where political father figures emerge as symbols or protégés of the revered patriarch. In turn, this resulted in the personalization of governance as exemplified by the Tourés, the Bandas, and the Mugabes. Invariably, it encouraged the sit-tight syndrome observed across the African political landscape from Sudan to Zimbabwe.

In addition, African political leaders are older than their counterparts from other parts of the world. For example, President Paul Biya of Cameroon is 87 years old, and he is not ready to hand the presidency over to the younger generation. Guinea's Alpha Conde is now 82, and Malawi's Peter Mutharika is 79. Some of these 'long-distance' men were aided to power and propped up by Western powers to serve their hegemonic interests in Africa.

As mentioned earlier, one common feature of political leadership in contemporary Africa is that it is neo-patrimonial, featuring clientelism, presidentialism, centralization of power, and the use of state resources for personal gains. In presidentialism, the political leader's authority is unopposed and unlimited. Here, state institutions exist in a symbolic rather than democratic form. A recent example of presidentialism is Zimbabwe, where the presidential power increased incrementally until the fall of Robert Mugabe in 2017 after 30 years. With his absolute power, Mugabe sidelined the Parliament, allowed periodic elections, but crushed any sign of political opposition.

Further, 'stayism' in the African political landscape relates to liberation movements-turned political parties. For instance, the Botswana Democratic Party (BDP) has continued to govern the country since independence in 1966. However, an exception must be made in the case of Botswana as it is Africa's longest-running democracy with a multi-party system and its citizens are among the wealthiest in the continent. Again, it must be noted that Botswana's House of

Traditional Leaders plays a crucial role in policy formulation and implementation.

Traditional Leadership in Sub-Saharan Africa

In Sub-Saharan Africa, traditional leadership is an integral part of the political system, although their appropriate role within the political landscape continues to be the subject of debate. Among these institutions, the Zulu kingdoms in South Africa (led by Goodwill Zwelithini) and the Ashanti in Ghana (led by the Asantehene, Osei Tutu II) remains the largest in terms of cultural dominance and political influence.

Unfortunately, many African liberation movements and subsequent post-liberation governments have emasculated and marginalized traditional authorities and leaders. Kwame Nkrumah, for instance, refused to include the Asantehene and other traditional leaders in his government. Also, President Nimeiri of Sudan in 1971 abolished the so-called native administration system and replaced it with regional and area councils. The same scenario also played out in many other African countries, from Burkina Faso to South Africa. In these cases, as noted by scholars, the failure of African political leaders to accommodate traditional leaders in the political system often led to disaster.

For instance, the removal of traditional institutions from the government in some African countries created a power vacuum, resulting in the militarization of ethnic groups. This, in turn, led to intractable inter-ethnic rivalries and clashes, which are endemic in the region. Ironically, as African political parties struggle with governance, they sometimes turn to traditional authorities for much-needed administrative and political support. In Ghana, Namibia,

Uganda, and Zimbabwe, traditional authorities have been duly recognized as the foundation of their political system. They are always consulted before important state policies are formulated.

Post-genocide Rwanda is a shining example of a country that has engrafted its traditional authorities into its current political structure and foisted on them the special task of managing the country's conflict resolution mechanisms. The country has over 60,000 Inyangamugayo (people of outstanding personality selected from each community) who act as volunteer conflict mediators in their various communities. The Sudanese peace agreement contains specific references to the key role traditional authorities could play in resolving the lingering conflict in the country. In contrast, Swaziland shows the dark side of traditional authority in Sub-Saharan Africa. Since 1973, the absolute monarch has banned opposition parties from participating in the nation's political system.

African Leadership Styles

A discussion of Sub-Saharan Africa's leadership situation is not complete without exploring the leadership styles adopted by the region's political leaders. Simply put, leadership style can be defined as a general concept that includes a leader's beliefs, decision-making methods, conflict resolution techniques, and typical ways of dealing with society. These leadership styles are relevant to our discussion because one style may yield an outcome different from the others.

First, the need for political power includes the apparent desire to influence and control people and groups. Like their forerunners, contemporary African political leaders are also concerned with establishing and maintaining their power and influence over others.

Closely related to the need mentioned earlier for political power are the various forms of corruption and nepotism that usually accompany it. A perverse system of "clientelism" or patronage operates whereby the state has the private sector as clients, and the political leaders have the state as their client. The resulting governments are neither here nor there and are often referred to by the international community as kleptocracies. We have seen examples of such systems of government in Chad, Cameroon, Congo DR, Nigeria, and Togo.

Secondly, as we know it, nationalism refers to a worldview in which one's nation is seen as superior to other nations or even exceptional. This imbues strong emotional ties to a person's country of birth, with a greater emphasis placed on national or ethnic identity. In Sub-Saharan Africa, this trait is manifested in attempts by political leaders to change the course of history and redefine the exceptionality of their country or ethnic group. This often resulted in myriads of ethnic conflicts and indigene/settler crises as witnessed in the Hutu/Tutsi clashes in Rwanda, the Sudanese war, the insurgency in Cameroon, the Biafran agitation in Nigeria, the Central African Republic crisis, the Hausa/Fulani conflicts in the Plateau State of Nigeria, and the ongoing crisis in Mali.

Furthermore, contemporary African political leadership has embraced a task-oriented approach to tackle the continent's governance issues. Specific task words like "African Renaissance," "African Recovery," "Great Rebirth," and others perfectly illustrate this trend. The establishment and implementation of significant initiatives like the African Union (AU), the African Peer Review Mechanism (APRM), and the New Partnership for Africa's Development (NEPAD) provide veritable examples. At the international level, African leaders are applying concepts and ideas such as nonalignment and Pan-Africanism. Here, we can identify Olusegun Obasanjo, Thabo Mbeki, and Paul Kagame as charismatic leaders with considerable political magnetism. Other proactive leaders are Ali Bongo, Hage Gottfried, and Macky Sall. These men have the political reputation for serving as models of what good leaders should be in Africa.

African Political Leaders' Paths to Power

Political leaders acquire their positions through ascription, appointment, nomination, ascension, election, or succession. Therefore, political leadership involves aspects of authority, legitimacy, influence, and power. Harold Lasswell explained that political leadership is essentially about power, how it is obtained, maintained, exercised, and legitimized. In this regard, political leadership in the Sub-Saharan African States can be categorized into three, namely: military, monarchical, and democratic.

Women as Political Leaders in Sub-Saharan Africa

In 2003, African countries, in unison, adopted the Protocol to the African Charter on Human and People's Rights on the Rights of Women in the continent. This clause seeks to improve the status of African women, promote gender equality, and end gender-based discrimination. Since that time, women's role in critical decision-making processes has seen some improvements. In 2004, Luisa Dias Diogo became the first Prime Minister of Mozambique. In 2005, Pumzile Mlambo-Ncguka was appointed the first female Deputy

President in South Africa. Marie-Angelique Savane was the chairperson of the APRM from 2003 to 2005. In 2004, Gertrude Mongella became the first speaker of the Pan-African Parliament through an election. In 2005, Liberia's Ellen Johnson-Sirleaf became the first elected female President in Africa. For Johnson-Sirleaf, her election undoubtedly sent a clear message of a growing need for alternative leadership styles in Africa aside from the old patrimonial system.

Furthermore, five of the ten members of the AU Commission in 2007 were women. From March 2021, Ngozi Okonjo-Iweala, a Nigerian economist and international development expert, was elected as Director-General of the World Trade Organization. She is the first woman and the first African to hold the office. Along the same line, Helen Zille was appointed the Premier of the Western Cape in South Africa. She was the leader of the Democratic Alliance, which is the only credible opposition to the nation's ruling party, the African National Congress (ANC). We also need to mention the exploits of Joyce Banda of Malawi, known for her outspoken views against corruption and bad governance and the protection of women's rights in Africa. She famously cancelled an AU summit in Malawi rather than allow President Omar al-Bashir of Sudan to attend.

Regional Solidarity in Africa

As for the question of leadership and regional solidarity in the African landscape, it would not be an exaggeration to say that it has been an African obsession during the first wave of independence in the 1960s. There is a consensus among politicians and scholars that

African solidarity in whatever form or shape is a question of necessity. Kwame Nkrumah, Ghana's first President, argued that Africa's leadership should take responsibility for rallying behind the cause of unity in the context of Africa's newly independent countries if they were to win the battle of development. He further lamented that "To go it alone will limit our horizons, curtail our expectations, and threaten our liberty." For him, only a continental government and an economic system would save Africa from impending doom.

Moreover, issues of economic development have become Africa's top priority, especially after the end of colonialism and the fall of the Berlin Wall in November 1991. The death of the Organization of African Unity (OAU) and its subsequent replacement with the African Union (AU) in 2002 could be seen in this light. It is the tragic expression of a people searching for the magic wand to solidarity one way or the other. Furthermore, remarks from observers of the African Continent all agree on the need for Africa to tilt the balance in favour of a united front. Hence, sub-Saharan Africa's political balkanization into arbitrary nation-states has continued to elicit from the region the understandable demand to restructure the fragmented zone into a more coherent and stronger economic and political entity.

What could be called Africa's new leadership had this concept in mind when setting up the New Partnership for Africa's Development (NEPAD). They also had the same idea in mind when they midwife and delivered the AU. The quest for solidarity and development is also expressed by creating many regional and sub-regional organizations in Africa, like the Southern African Development Community (SADC) and the Economic Community of West African States (ECOWAS).

In the recent past, Apartheid, as rightly proclaimed, dealt a severe infringement blow on human rights. This made the UN classify

Apartheid as a crime against humanity. At that time, the UN Secretary-General was moved to declare that a country's sovereignty should be superseded by universal sovereignty in such cases. The Apartheid regime in South Africa witnessed this twist in international diplomacy within and outside Africa. The global campaign, led by the UN Committee and the worldwide Anti-Apartheid Movement, became increasingly interventionist in nature as different measures, such as economic sanctions, an arms embargo, and cultural boycotts, were instituted on many fronts to weaken the Apartheid regime and strengthen South African liberation movements. Such international solidarity or interventionist campaigns have been replicated in Mali (against Islamic terrorists), Nigeria, Chad, and Cameroon (against Boko Haram), Sudan (against ethnic militias), the Central African Republic (against ethnic warlords), Congo DR (against ethnic militias), etc.

Moreover, numerous African leaders of the new millennium, including Olusegun Obasanjo, Thabo Mbeki, and Paul Kagame, have shown a significant interest in regional and international affairs. Since realizing that it can make a considerable impact by championing regional solidarity within the continent, South Africa has continued to exert its influence in multilateral and regional organizations to work towards a democratic international order. In this regard, South Africa's landmark achievements include the global campaign to ban blood diamonds in Sierra Leone, Guinea, and Liberia (through the Kimberley Process), anti-personnel mines, and its efforts towards nuclear disarmament.

Also, South Africa's ability to assume a leadership position and generate initiatives in Africa has enabled the nation to act as a voice for the whole of Africa. Other verifiable demonstrations of its leadership capability include its contribution to the establishment of the New African Initiative (NAI), its involvement in the Inter-Congolese Dialogue (ICD), The New Partnership for Africa's Development (NEPAD), the Millennium African Recovery Plan (MAP), and other laudable projects.

The politics of solidarity is also evident in the high levels of contribution provided by Nigerian leaders like Olusegun Obasanjo, Musa Yar'adua, and Goodluck Jonathan in fostering peace in West Africa via peacekeeping operations in such places as Guinea, Liberia, Sierra Leone, and Mali. These leaders embraced opportunities provided by multilateral organizations such as the ECOWAS and the AU to promote peace in their sub-region.

Also, we have seen new commitments to introduce fresh initiatives and norms to address African states' concerns and existing concerns about the marginalization of Africa. Here, South Africa continues to set the pace in playing the role of a bridge-builder between the industrialized West and Sub-Saharan Africa. Examples of this bridge-building role could be seen in the Free Trade Development and Cooperative Agreement (FTDCA) with the European Union (EU) and its economic relations with the US concerning the African Growth and Opportunities Act (AGOA).

It could be argued that emerging regional solidarity among African countries is based on mutual feelings of community solidarity, loyalty, and deep concern for the welfare and fate of others. Thus, this trend suggests that Africa and Africans may soon break free from the shackles of neocolonialism, which have held them back from identifying with a common cause.

Challenges to Political Leadership in Sub-Saharan Africa

In Sub-Saharan Africa, leadership and authority are often backed up by coercive power. Hence, authority is usually located in a 'compliance-defiance' ideology, whereby compliance indicates the following types of authority: affiliative authority, knowledge authority, issue-specific authority, moral authority, and reputational authority. In stark contrast, defiance occurs where balance is lacking between the people's expectations and needs, on one hand, and that of specific individuals in positions of authority, on the other hand.

Challenges to political leadership and authority in the region include political instability, inter-ethnic rivalry, corruption, religious superstition and fanaticism, illiteracy, etc. A public authority in Sub-Saharan Africa can be divided into moral and illegitimate authority. A clash of these types of authority is responsible for religious terrorism in places like Nigeria, Niger, Chad, Somalia, and Mali. Reasons for this include:

- Contemporary terrorism in Africa operates within the ambits of international and local networks that seek to overthrow existing political systems.

- The emergence of terrorist groups, suicide attacks, global terrorist networks that are less dependent on state sponsorship, and the introduction of high-grade military weapons are geared towards the enthronement of Islamic rule.

Conclusion

This chapter will be concluded by a brief discussion of emerging trends in the African political landscape. A recent phenomenon in the region is African leaders' goals of providing task-oriented leadership. Whereas liberation from colonial rule was the primary goal of the earlier generation of African leaders, the most significant post-Cold War development has been efforts channelled towards greater regional integration.

Ambitious regional proposals and the ideas of a 'United States of Africa' were first muted by Pan-Africanists like Leopold Senghor, Kwame Nkrumah, and William du Bois. Despite numerous challenges and setbacks, the Pan-African and subcontinental organizations such as the AU (formerly OAU), the East African Community (EAC), the Southern African Development Commission (SADC), the Economic Community of Central African States (ECCAS), and the Economic Community of West African States (ECOWAS) still recorded notable achievements. For instance, the OAU's raison d'etre was the decolonization of Africa and the abolition of Apartheid in South Africa - which were eventually achieved. Since the 1990s, the OAU and other continental initiatives have undergone various reforms to fulfil their policy objectives. OAU became AU, and it has the mandate to tackle Africa's development problems. Also, the formation of NEPAD from NAI in 2001 attests to the new political will of African political leaders to promote African ownership and to take responsibility to protect democracy and human rights throughout the region.

2

A FOREIGNER'S VIEW: DEBUNKING THE MISCONCEPTIONS

Chapter 2

They themselves mocked Africa, trading stories of absurdity, of stupidity, and they felt safe to mock because it was a mockery born of longing and of the heartbroken desire to see a place made whole again

– Chimamanda Adichie

It is not altogether surprising that foreigners have many misconceptions and myths about leadership in Sub-Saharan Africa. Most times, African leadership is viewed through only the narrow prism of Western principles and theories and portrayed negatively, thus forgetting that leadership, of any type, is contextual and subject to societal dynamics.

In this chapter, we go-ahead to undertake a reassessment of several myths held by foreigners about leadership in Africa; the chapter debunks these myths and clears the air on the lopsided view of African leadership. Simultaneously, efforts will be made to paint an accurate picture of the situation of things in the region.

The Past as Prologue

In pre-colonial Africa, there were strong leadership institutions and structures that enabled the growth and development of the region, with advanced political systems recorded in the Songhai Empire, Benin Empire, the Oyo Empire, the Habe kingdoms, Bornu Empire, Mali Empire, Kongo Kingdom, and the Aksumite Empire. Studies of these ancient African kingdoms revealed evidence of systematic succession plans, which demanded accountability and good governance from the leaders, with the inherent risk of being ridiculed and forced to surrender by the people if there was a vote of no confidence.

In the colonial era, leaders of Sub-Saharan African became mere pawns on the chessboard of the European colonialists who seemed more interested in exploiting the region and carting away its God-given resources than genuinely developing the place. To achieve their aim, they empowered leaders who served their selfish interests instead of consolidating the existing leadership structures.

One of the most important findings to emerge from the study conducted on the leadership approaches and practices of five racial or societal groups, including Western, Afrikaner, African, Indian, and Jewish, is that contrary to what Western scholars and other social commentators have preached over the years, African societies possessed highly dynamic leadership styles in history. Granted that they have regressed and continued to suffer from lack of mastery of science and technology, African societies had, until it was disrupted by the scourge of colonialism, a highly effective leadership system that was backed by traditional philosophies, customs, and rituals.

According to the mindsets and value-judgments already ingrained in their minds as foreign explorers, conquerors, and exploiters, Africa's leadership problems started when colonialists sought to interpret its leadership systems and societal institutions. So, what they did not understand was dismissed as primitive, and they proceeded to tear down the structures or try to replace them with their conceptions of what should be.

In post-colonial Africa, the newly empowered struggle leaders who had no prior leadership experience of leading large groups of people simply faltered and floundered. They failed to appreciate the enormity of their tasks, and in a bid to exert their authority and appear to be strong leaders, those at the helm of affairs resorted to using coercive force to control their people and consolidate their hold on power. The actions of the first sets of post-colonial African leaders, more than anything else, have been responsible for the skewed perspectives of the global community about leadership in Africa.

The inaccurate descriptions and interpretations given to African leadership structures led to the development of some perfidious leadership myths, which have been in circulation among Western scholars and the international media community. As the eminent African scholar, Masango stated, "Developed countries have always viewed Africa as a place plagued by corruption, nepotism, dictatorship, military coups, rebellious leaders, greediness, misuse of power, incompetent leadership, politically motivated assassinations, politically, as well as economically ineffective and suspicious leaders who undermine their own democracies." Hence, it is imperative to look at some of the leadership myths about Sub-Saharan Africa and present the true picture of things.

Misconceptions and Truths about Leadership in Sub-Saharan Africa

1. African leaders are generally corrupt

While it is true that corruption is endemic and rampant in many Sub-Saharan African countries, it is still not exclusive to the region. It can be argued that African leaders learnt corruption from their former colonial masters. Besides, there are many countries in Africa, such as Botswana and Rwanda, where corruption is not tolerated. The governments of these countries are known for the giant strides they have made in the last decade in providing exemplary leadership for their people and making significant changes in the polity.

Further, Sub-Saharan Africa has also experienced transformational leadership. Former President of South Africa, Nelson Mandela, won the Nobel Peace Prize in 1993 for his laudable contributions to the Anti-Apartheid Movement and his statesmanlike approach to politics after winning the presidential election in 1994. Also, three women, two of them Africans, won the Nobel Peace Prize in 2011. President Ellen Johnson-Sirleaf of Liberia and Leymah Gbowee, also of Liberia, were awarded prizes for their international intervention efforts to resolve the second Liberian Civil War.

2. Leadership in Sub-Saharan Africa is masculine

Many foreigners have this misconception that contact with Western civilization brought about the struggle for women's rights in Sub-Saharan African societies. But Africans have always had strong women leaders who played notable roles in the history of their communities. In African oral history, for instance, there are numerous stories of Amazons who, as individuals or groups of women, led their clans as rulers and fought against injustice, wanting the best for their people.

In the pre-colonial era, Ethiopia's Queen Amanirenas ruled the ancient kingdom around 332 BCE and was famous for her military prowess and leadership skills. Also, Queen Amina of Zaria (in present-day Nigeria) was known as a warrior who possessed unquestionable leadership skills, and she expanded the territory of her Hausa kingdom. The old kingdom of Dahomey in the present-day Benin Republic also had a regiment of fearsome female warriors known as the "Amazons of Dahomey," who fought gallantly in all the wars prosecuted by their kingdom in the 18th and 19th centuries.

In addition, the colonial era saw the active participation of African women leaders in fighting off foreign invaders and oppressive colonialists. An excellent example of this is seen in the case of Queen Nzingha of Angola, who held off the Portuguese colonialists for 30 years. Another notable woman who stood her ground against European colonization was Queen Yaa Asantewa of Ghana's old Ashanti Empire. She encouraged her people to fight for the freedom of the abducted King Prempeh while turning down the overtures of the invaders.

But it was not only women in high places of authority who showcased their laudable leadership skills during the colonial era in Sub-Saharan Africa. In 1921, there was the Aba Women Riot in Nigeria. It was, in summary, an anti-colonial uprising led by everyday Nigerian women in the Eastern Nigerian city of Aba, who expressed their anger over various social, economic, and political injustices dished out by the British colonialists. A few decades later, in 1940, Nigeria again witnessed a revolt led by women against dehumanizing colonial policies. Known as the Egba Women Tax Riot, it was a brainchild of the Abeokuta Women's Union, which had Mrs. Funmilayo Ransome Kuti (the mother of the legendary Afrobeat superstar, Fela Anikulapo Kuti) as one of its champions. The campaign was to protest the imposition of unfair taxes on Nigerian women by the British colonial administration.

These stories and numerous others show that leadership in Sub-Saharan Africa was much more sophisticated and dynamic than Western scholars often wrote in their history textbooks and journals. African women, in many respects, lived fulfilled lives before the coming of the colonialists. Women were accorded with due respect, and they were given prime roles in the political affairs of their communities. There was hardly any African traditional political system in which women did not hold important chieftaincy titles. They were also deeply engaged in the social and economic matters of their clans, as they played notable roles in the day-to-day running of the community.

Yet, African women have not stopped canvassing for their rights and those of their people. Today's generation of African amazons has continued to occupy exalted positions in the business, economic and political world, just as their ancestors did in the past. For instance, Sub-Saharan Africa has produced four female presidents, something the United States is yet to achieve. They are President Catherine Samba-Panza of the Central African Republic, Amreenah Gurib-Fakum of Mauritius, Ellen Johnson-Sirleaf of Liberia, and Joyce Banda of Malawi. The most unbelievable story is Rwanda in 2020, when 62% of the nation's national legislators were women, thus setting a global standard.

Beyond taking up the highest executive office as presidents and prime ministers, women are also present in their country's national parliaments, becoming cabinet ministers, deputy ministers, state or regional governors, chief judges, and holding top positions in all arms of government.

Nigeria's former Finance Minister, Ngozi Okonjo-Iweala, and Namibia's Netumbo Nandi-Ndaitwah are two of Africa's most influential political actors. And they are women. One must not forget the appointment of Nkosazana Dlamini-Zuma as the President of the AU Commission in 2013. This unexpected and likely trend reflects the receptiveness of African society to women occupying leadership positions.

3. Sub-Saharan African leadership is dominated by big men and gerontocracy

As he prepared to step down as Tanzania's President in 2005, Benjamin Mkapa called for a new home-grown democracy in Africa. He said, "That Africa ended up with big men at the State House is entirely unrelated to this colonial legacy. Colonialists did not prepare Africans for a self-democratic rule."

Together with the notion that African leadership is masculine, the myth of big men is another ill-conceived opinion of foreigners about leadership in the region. There is this mistaken belief that one needs to have connections with powerful cabals or godfathers to succeed in both politics and business within Africa. The Western media generally apply the Big Man epithet only to African leaders. Some have traced its roots to the colonialists and their actions when selecting pliant rulers to succeed them in Africa after independence.

While it is quite true that some leaders rise to the top this way in many countries, including the developed countries such as the United States, where their presidential candidates have to solicit rich and powerful individuals for endorsements, as well as for campaign finances, this is not the whole story. The truth is that many Africans with no connections or links to some big man or godfather are increasingly carving out a niche for themselves and beating their path to the top in various human endeavours.

Luckily, a new generation of responsible political leaders is sprouting on the African landscape. Young people such as Hlomela, South Africa's youngest MP, and Eddy Oketch Gicheru (a young Kenyan and MasterCard Foundation Scholar who ran for the Senate in the 2018 Kenyan general elections) are already coming through with fresh perspectives.

In almost every African society, respect for the elderly is a strong norm in their socio-behavioural code. So, before Moses wrote his Ten Commandments enjoining the Israelites to honour their parents and, by extension, the elderly, as a requisite to having a long life, Africans already knew about respect and honour for their elders. Honour and respect for the elderly are so entrenched in African consciousness that it sometimes seems that Africans practice gerontocracy - the rule by older adults. This misconception has been promoted by a set of mythologies, which do not reflect the true picture of youth involvement in leadership at every level of the African social strata.

4. Power change in Sub-Saharan Africa is always violent

This myth is another misconception about Sub-Saharan Africa's leadership landscape. However, the African political landscape was once dominated by military coups, sit-tight rulers, and election violence. When voters think there has been electoral fraud, the risk of an election-related crisis is always high. In some cases, the violence is instigated by influential leaders who feel threatened by the opposition.

Table 1: Regime types in sub-Saharan African countries until 1989.

One-party system	Military oligarchies	Competitive one-party systems	Multi-party systems
Angola, Benin, Cape Verde, Comoros, Congo, Djibouti, Equatorial Guinea, Ethiopia, Gabon, Guinea Bissau, Kenya, Mozambique, Niger, Somalia, Swaziland, Zaire	Burkina Faso, Burundi, Chad, Guinea, Lesotho, Liberia, Mauritania, Nigeria, Sudan, Uganda	Cameroon, Central African Republic, Cote d'Ivoire, Madagascar, Mali, Malawi, Rwanda, Sao Tome, Seychelles, Sierra Leone, Tanzania, Togo, Zambia	Botswana, Gambia, Mauritius, Senegal, Zimbabwe.

Source: Bratton and Van de Wallet (1993)

Table 2: Military coups in Africa since independence (regional statistics)

Region	1950s/ 1960s	1970s	1980s	1990s	2000s	2010s	Total
North Africa	7	1	4	1	2	2	17
Sub-Saharan Africa	22	21	16	13	4	4	80
Total	29	22	20	14	6	6	97

However, there has been considerable improvement in recent decades. The region now experiences peaceful political transitions to power almost every year, while the elections in Africa that most attract Western media attention are often those that turn out violent. But many more are generally peaceful. Nigeria's former President, Dr Goodluck Jonathan, provided a great example, who conceded defeat in the 2015 general elections and handed the presidency over to the incumbent President, Muhammadu Buhari, without any violence or bloodletting. A similar scenario also played out in Ghana between former President John Dramani Mahama and the current President, Nana Akufo-Addo, in 2017. South Africa, Malawi, and Liberia are some of the other African countries where peaceful elections have become a routine. These occurrences have simply debunked the notion that power transitions in Sub-Saharan Africa are always violent.

5. Sub-Saharan African Leadership is democratic deficit

Many countries grapple with democratic deficits from Canada to Uganda. Yet, this popular notion that Sub-Saharan African countries lag behind the rest of the world is nebulous of political concepts. Even though billions of people elsewhere in the world live under regimes that can best be described as authoritarian, oppressive, and undemocratic, for instance, China and Russia operate home-grown communist systems. Yet, derogatory labels are not hung on their leaders. Besides, the former British Prime Minister, Winston Churchill, once thought democracy was "the worst form of government, except for all the others." Coming from a so-called home of democracy, his words reflect the imperfections of what we call democracy and lay bare how difficult it is to define.

Furthermore, countries that describe themselves as democracies are members of a not-so-exclusive broad church. They range from nations that protect fundamental human rights and civil liberties to those that repress the opposition and hold elections that are neither free nor fair. At the same time, it is true that a club of authoritarian leaders once held sway across Sub-Saharan Africa, either by repressing the opposition and civil society or by amending the constitution to extend their tenures in office. Of course, these African countries were not in any way alone in this. For example, Lee Kuan Yew, the founding father of Singapore, led the country for more than three decades and his human rights records were not outstanding. More so, Cambodia's Hun Sen has also been in power for 35 years, and in Kazakhstan, Nursultan Nazarbayev was in power from 1990 to March 2019.

Just as other regions of the world have various governance systems, there are apparent discrepancies among African states. According to the Economist Intelligence Unit's Democracy Index, the four categories of African political system and leadership succession patterns include full democracy, flawed democracy, authoritarian, and a hybrid of the first three. In its 2015 index, there was uneven progress across Sub-Saharan Africa, but a dramatic drop in successful military coups since 2000, as shown in Table 2. In the region, only nine leaders have been in power for more than two decades; three of them have been at the helm of affairs for more than three decades.

Some countries have defied the narrative of a democratic deficit in African leadership, however. In the 2016 Freedom in the World publication, Freedom House listed Cote d'Ivoire, South Africa, Nigeria, and Liberia among African countries with significant civil liberties and political rights improvements. As mentioned earlier, Sub-Saharan African countries such as Benin, Cape Verde, Botswana, Ghana, and Nigeria, have all witnessed democratic power shifts within the leadership cadre. Aside from the increasing number of leaders relinquishing power peacefully after election defeats, there have been several cases of popular uprisings against leaders who attempted to extend their tenures, such as Zimbabwe's Robert Mugabe, Malawi's Bakili Muluzi, and Zambia's Frederick Chiluba. In 2014, Burkina Faso's Blaise Compaoré's bid to prolong his 27-year rule was thwarted by a violent revolt. President Pierre Nkurunziza's successful bid to extend his term in office sparked a crisis in Burundi.

Millions of people across Africa enjoy the benefits of relatively good governance provided by transformational leaders such as Paul Kagame and Joyce Banda. In the year 2020 alone, not less than 10 Sub-Saharan African countries held their presidential elections. Although periodic elections do not automatically translate to representative governments and democratic leadership, yet multi-party politics is still a sine qua non for democracy. Regular elections indicate progress towards ensuring that citizens can democratically choose their leaders.

6. **It is more difficult for African leaders to succeed in global leadership roles**: The fact is that there is a split verdict on the probability of success of African leaders in global leadership roles. The reality is that African leaders can at least be as successful as their Western counterparts in international roles. A notable example was Kofi Annan, as the UN Secretary-General from 1997 to 2006. He was also a co-recipient with the UN of the 2001 Nobel Peace Prize.

Similarly, the story of Dr Akinwunmi Adesina, President of the African Development Bank (AfDB), continues to show that a new breed of African leaders can effectively lead international organizations. But who is he?

Adesina, 60, is a distinguished development expert with 27 years of international experience at the Alliance for a Green Revolution in Africa (AGRA) and the Rockefeller Foundation in New York. He also served as a Principal Economist at the International Institute of Tropical Agriculture (IITA) and the International Crop Research Institute for the Semi-Arid Tropics (ICRISAT) at one time or another. He was also the Nigerian Minister of Agriculture from 2010 to 2015, during which he introduced many reforms in the Nigerian Agricultural Sector. Above all, he was named Person of the Year by Forbes Africa magazine in 2013.

Needless to say, that he has an enviable record working in international organizations for over 20 years. For this reason, many commentators saw the recent American-led opposition to Adesina's second term bid at AfDB as another manifestation of Western imperialism in Africa. Some scholars argued that the issue stemmed from his purported pro-China stance, having angered the "Americans" and promoting agricultural domestication in Nigeria, rubbing off badly on American agribusiness interests. Others have hinted about a dark and sinister plot to derail Africa's financial progress and impose Western hegemony on the continent through the back door of hostage finance. As further evidence of this "geopolitical agenda" to damage Adesina's reputation, different commentators point to recent comments by David Malpass, President of the World Bank, criticizing the AfDB for lax credit standards purportedly driving profligate African leaders towards debt distress.

Whatever the case, the recent upheaval at the AfDB seems to be another case of geopolitical skullduggery and an attempt by a Western country, America this time, to dictate African policies. After all, the AfDB Investigative Panel set up to review the allegations of misconduct, found Adesina not guilty, and acquitted him of all charges.

However, there are numerous constraints around global leadership opportunities for African leaders because large enterprises tend to be homogeneous at the senior level and Western nations have greater power over major international organizations.

Conclusion

Sub-Saharan African is one of the largest and most significant geopolitical zones of the world and one of the most misunderstood. Even though there is a lot of improvement, it is still safe to say that the region isn't only about the version shown on the BBC, CNN, or DW. SSA has been developing over time. From Lagos to Addis Ababa, a new breed of leaders is coming up with more developmental initiatives. Hence, despondency is gradually giving way to renewed hope. So far, I have debunked some myths by foreigners about the African leadership landscape.

Let's now explore indigenous African institutions to see if Africa's current leaders can learn one or two lessons from Africa's past.

3

INDIGENOUS AFRICAN INSTITUTIONS: A WALKTHROUGH TIMES AND EVENTS

Chapter 3

Those who close their eyes to facts will learn through accidents

– African Proverb

Figure 2: Ethnographic map of Africa. Source: Meyers Blitz Lexikon (1932)

Africa's developmental challenge remains a source of worry to its people and concerned scholars all over the world. Part of efforts to address this problem has been studies of the region's institutions - past and present, and their legacies for both economic and political development. Most of these researches have focused on the role of colonial rule - the structural packages that European powers put in place across Africa from the 16th to 20th century. Indeed, there are good reasons to focus on colonialism's effect on institutional development in African countries. For one, colonial rule was a profoundly disruptive adventure that radically altered how African societies were structured. Important factors such as the operation of the law, the nature of taxation, trade, and leadership institutions were significantly impacted. Moreover, colonialism engulfed almost all countries of sub-Saharan Africa except for Ethiopia, thus making it a primary source of exogenous variation of institutional quality in the region.

Though the importance of colonialism is highly recognized in this context, recent studies have increasingly highlighted a prominent role for pre-colonial institutions in the current dispensation. Many of these studies have rightly focused on sub-Saharan Africa with particular reference to parts of the continent where colonialists arrived late (African hinterlands were mostly unknown to Europeans till the late 1800s) and did not last long (African countries gained independence within a century of colonization), except for countries in southern Africa. Given these conditions, it is not entirely surprising that pre-colonial institutions transcend the colonial era and continue to shape African societies to this day. Therefore, recent studies have extended to the anthropological study of African societies to look beyond the colonial era to trace the legacies of indigenous pre-colonial institutions in Sub-Saharan Africa.

If anything, such studies have signalled a welcome shift away from the undue emphasis on the relatively brief period of colonial rule.

However, it has become controversial for some reasons. One has been the debate about how reliable these researchers report on the pre-colonial era. Another controversy hinges on how pre-colonial institutions could be reformulated to engender African development in the long run. Despite these controversies, it is still widely acknowledged that the colonial era was too brief an era to study African leadership institutions. Even though the era saw the creation of many of the existing national boundaries and the superimposition of alien legal structures, which have somehow survived the transition to independence, this era was still characterized by considerable socio-political turmoil with ugly occurrences, which renders it inappropriate to be solely used for studying indigenous leadership styles. Hence, we intend to go further in time to examine the pre-colonial political structures in Africa to see if we can learn one or two things therein. For the sake of clarity and decompression of research, however, the chapter adopts an axial approach to studying West Africa first; then, East and Southern Africa will follow suit. Where necessary, we shall delve briefly into African history to let the readers see how things were done before colonization.

Pre-colonial Political Experience in Africa

There is significant evidence of diversity in political experience across sub-Saharan Africa before the advent of colonialism. At one extreme, there were societies with centralized organization and hierarchical administrative systems, such as the Luba Kingdom in Central Africa, the Songhai Empire in West Africa, and the Kingdom of Buganda in Eastern Africa. At the other extreme were decentralized systems without central political heads beyond the village level, which were seen among the Konkomba in Ghana and Togo, the Igbo, Ibibio, and

Tiv in Nigeria, the Fulani in the Sahel and West Africa, the Tallensi in northern Ghana, the Chakali of Ghana's Upper West Region, the Nuer in Sudan, and the Somali in the Horn of Africa. At the middle of the spectrum is occupied by those societies organized in loose alliances and large chiefdoms such as the Wolof and the Ewe in West Africa. While the latter societies lacked statehood in the actual sense, they still had a somewhat centralized decision-making process and conflict-resolution mechanisms.

When everything is considered, it is revealed that colonial rule impacted these ancient political structures. The main reason being that the colonialists sought to replace indigenous institutions with imported structures alien to the indigenous societies of Sub-Saharan Africa. So, they did everything to undermine African leaders and to sow seeds of distrust in the polity. It is also true that even after independence, some African countries attempted to reduce the role of indigenous institutions. But Africans themselves have continued to rely on ethno-specific structures rather than the state due to many African governments' inability to provide good governance across the board. For instance, while newly independent countries like Chad, Niger, and Mozambique initially attempted to marginalize local chiefs, they quickly shelved the Policy due to great difficulties experienced in governing the rural areas.

Furthermore, old ethnic institutions of kingship and chiefdom continue to enjoy considerable support and popularity among the African populace. Also, these chiefs still wield significant powers in the enforcement of customary laws and land allocation rights. Thus, there is an urgent need to explore these pre-colonial institutions as a way of refuting claims that Africans had no exemplary leadership institutions before the advent of colonialism.

While it is true that we still have more to learn about how leadership structures evolved in Africa, the legacies of pre-colonial political institutions are hard to overlook. In all cases, agriculturally productive environments, opportunities for local and inter-ethnic cooperation, and leadership initiatives drawing from various power modes contributed to the process. Pre-colonial states across the region were characterized by the intensification of socio-political hierarchy, long-distance exchange, territorial expansion and integration, the promulgation of state policies, and leadership succession plans.

Evidence abounds to suggest that in each African geopolitical zone, political leaders drew from a range of local cultural resources in crafting political ideologies, which resulted in a diverse set of state forms across the region. Besides, sub-Saharan African archaeological endeavours grew in the late 19th and early 20th centuries, simultaneously with the expansion of European colonialism across the region. Those European explorers, missionaries, and merchants met thriving kingdoms and various legacies of ancient civilizations.

African civilizations, defined in terms of a set of identifiable characteristics (architecture, irrigation agriculture, divine kingship, metallurgy, monumental art, and others), were mischievously cast as the products of cultural progress incubated elsewhere, a myth that reinforced the hegemonic logic of European colonialists in Africa. Except for ancient civilizations along the Horn and the Nile Valley, evidence for early contact between sub-Saharan Africa and the Near East has been relatively limited and sparse.

In further response to such notions, African scholars have also explored a diverse set of case studies, more closely experimenting with analytical concepts to further explain the variable nature of political authority within the complexity of local cultures. These studies have accommodated the role of indigenous leadership institutions in shaping the political landscape of pre-colonial cultures across Africa, showing significant diversity in both the origins and legacies of state formation over the last five millennia.

As stated earlier, there is a myriad of evidence that Africa was not an uncontrollable region peopled by savages during the pre-colonial era. For instance, African chiefs were accountable to their communities through intra-community assemblies. While these chiefs were powerful, there were still checks and balances to checkmate them in the event of perceived or real excesses. Anthropologists and archaeologists had detected similar pre-colonial power arrangements on their field trips across Africa. Their findings revealed that Africa in pre-colonial times was primarily governed by a lineage (hereditary) kingship system in which bureaucracy was limited.

Pre-colonial leadership in Africa could be described as a marriage between popular democracy and autocratic dictatorship. Cultural practices vary slightly from one culture to another, which allowed erring chiefs to be sanctioned by their followers, and they could even be rejected as leaders. This was noticed in certain cultures in the Cameroons, where new leaders had to go through an initiation ritual of stoning to confirm acceptance or rejection by the people. Little pebbles would be used if the leader was accepted, and large stones, if otherwise.

During this period, Africa had a set of leadership selection criteria based mainly on indigenous culture. In some societies, leadership selection was divine and hereditary as it is passed on to the heir (most senior son), and in other cultures, it was based on seniority. In cases where there were many eligible candidates, the selection process was often based on divination. A deity would be consulted to prophesy accurately about the future. The outcomes were usually acceptable to all since the collective aspiration of the community was deemed much more important to the people than the transient reign of rulers. Whenever there was a bad leader, people had the power to ask the ruler to surrender, or the ruler would be sent into exile or forced to commit suicide.

While it is true that pre-colonial African leaders were powerful and enjoyed absolute authority to demand obedience, their power was often moderated either by some rituals or a council of chiefs to avoid abuse of power. This kind of arrangement was seen among Cameroonian cultures, Botswana tribal groups, and in Oyo Empire. Although the Alaafin (king) of Oyo Empire was very powerful, his powers were checked by the interventions of the privy council of the Oyo Mesi (comprising the Bashorun - Prime Minister; Agbaakin - High Priest of Oranmiyan; Samu - Sacrificial Minister; Alapini - High Priest of Egungun; Laguna - Roving Ambassador; Akiniku - Chief of Defence Staff; and Ashipa - Mayor of the Imperial Capital) and the subordinate Ogboni Earth Cult of noblemen. Several Alaafins were forced to commit suicide by Bashorun Gaa -- the traditional prime minister of Oyo - in the late 1700s.

The effectiveness of pre-colonial leadership structures in Africa is shown by the simple fact that when British colonial rule came to these areas, they had to govern indirectly by relying on the old administrative and political systems or structures. The colonialists did not foolishly apply the indirect rule to all her colonies uniformly but acknowledged every culture's uniqueness. To streamline their colonial rule, the British government adopted three approaches. Firstly, they recognized and appointed some educated individuals as representatives of their people. This approach was adopted in places where there were educated local elites. The appointment was made so that only people who enjoyed popular support were selected to the native council. Such educated persons had to satisfy three criteria, namely: popularity among the people, ability to speak the local language, and being well-versed in the customs of their community. The second approach was to grant local chiefs unfettered authority over their people. The last approach was to grant those communities that were politically sophisticated greater authority for self-governance. Such powers were gradually increased with the ultimate aim of granting those places complete autonomy, as seen in the Egba United Nations. Under this arrangement, power was granted to local chiefs to impose taxes, but the British government monitored its use. This unique approach appreciated each local chief's ability and adapted the control mechanism to suit the situation. In some Nigerian communities, north and south, the kings and their traditional councils were granted absolute authority over their subjects.

Early Signs of Statehood in West Africa

In the western part of Africa, trading empires and kingdoms emerged possibly due to rising global trade in the late first to early second millennium AD. From Mali to Morocco, nomadic pastoralists travelled across the Sahara from the fourth millennium BC, leaving behind clear evidence of an emerging socio-political hierarchy in the form of differential access to luxury goods such as beads and bracelets, as well as barrow burials for the dead. By the early second to the late first millennia BC, some of the ancient elites had started experimenting with larger-scale socio-political integration, as shown by multi-layered settlement hierarchies, including those found at the

Dhar Tichitt archaeological site in southern Mauritania and other places.

Moreover, the West African Sahel offered opportunities for the emergence of African states in the precolonial period due primarily to its closeness to the lucrative trans-Saharan trade. According to scholars, by the first millennium CE, there were already tell-tale signs of settlement nucleation and large-scale urbanism in the inland Niger-Delta region of Mali. Scholars have suggested that these communities relied on hierarchical political and social integration. Others can rule any unit based on circumstances, and no one unit dominates the others.

However, the advent of Islam and the increasing demand for resources from Sub-Saharan Africa in the Near East and North Africa in the late first millennium CE led to a reconfiguration of the region's political landscape so that heterarchical communities began to be incorporated into hierarchical militaristic empires and kingdoms, linking forest belt, Sahelian, and Near Eastern communities together in a complex web. For example, whereas the Soninke Kingdom of Ghana (present-day Mali and southeast Mauritania) had developed centralized kingship by the middle of the first millennium CE, its rapid expansion from the 10th to the 12th centuries was attributable to its trans-Saharan trading networks.

Furthermore, the fall of the Mali Empire (13th to 15th centuries), the Songhai (14th to 16th centuries), and the Sayfawa State of Kanem-Bornu (from 16th to 17th centuries), as well as the Hausa states of northern Nigeria (13th to 19th centuries), followed a similar pattern of elite attempts to build states that dramatically imposed socio-political complexity on local communities within their territories. Nevertheless, many indigenous communities such as the Igbo and

Ibibio in West Africa maintained their heterarchical principles of the political organization till they made contact with European colonialists later in the day.

Moving down south in West Africa's forest belt, iron-producing agrarian communities began transforming the natural vegetation into a string of centralized states by 1000 CE. From this period, Akan towns started to emerge along the northern fringes of modern Ghana. Under similar circumstances in Nigeria's forest zone to the south, important urban civilizations, including the Ife Kingdom of the Yorubas, emerged. Toward the coast, similar factors saw the emergence of the Benin Empire and the Ijebu Kingdom as centralized states under distinct rulers. The Yoruba-Edo states' political centres were specifically marked by sophisticated leadership structures that integrated corporate groups, towns, chiefdoms, and villages into a web of regional hierarchies. Across the River Niger to the east, the Igbos and their Arochukwu Confederacy, including the Igbos, the Efiks, and Ibibios, were located with their unique decentralized political system.

Early Signs of Statehood in East and Southern Africa

Toward the coast in East Africa (from Mozambique to Ethiopia), major indigenous political centres flourished between the 8th and 15th centuries CE. Various Bantu, Ethiopian, and Swahili communities, including Gedi, Kilwa Kisiwani, Manda, Msiri, Shanga, Ethiopia, Monomatapa, Funj, and Merina, were characterized by a political elite corps and marked by elaborate palace structures surrounded by vast wattle structures built by commoners. Numerous archaeological findings have since debunked the idea that the Swahili civilization, or any of those mentioned, were introduced from the Near East rather than a product of the gradual evolution of indigenous Bantu settlements. There is overwhelming evidence that Swahili cities emerged within dynamic settlement landscapes of Bantu origins.

The international style of status distinction, materialized by contact with foreign cultures, rarely penetrated the Swahili hinterland, thus indicating the emergence of a social divide between urban and rural communities across the landscape. Howbeit, coastal cities were still interconnected with the rural countryside in complex economic and political mosaics involving mobile pastoralists, settled farmers, hunter-gatherers, and urban elites. The result was a maze of strong yet geographically restricted city-states ruled by a cosmopolitan elite that dominated maritime trade in East Africa until the arrival of the Portuguese in the 15th century.

In southern Africa, the Zimbabwe plateau offered a pleasant, well-watered, and fertile environment suitable for agriculture, pastoralism, and human settlement and proximity to the source of valuable goods (gold and ivory), which was highly in demand on the coast. Archaeological field trips have provided evidence of early experiments in socio-political complexity in the Shashi-Limpopo confluence. The sites of K-2, Mapungubwe, and Schroda showed the emergence of a rain-making cult at the principal centres as early as the 8th to the 13th centuries CE, which possibly deepened settlement hierarchy and expressions of social status on a regional scale. At Mapungubwe, for instance, these interactions culminated in the rise of a class-based city-state administered on the principles of divine leadership, which declined in the 13th century due to unfavourable climatic conditions and other local influences.

Between the 13th century and the 16th century, similar Shona-speaking cultures on the Zimbabwe plateau somehow wrested control of the lucrative gold and ivory trade from the Mapungubwe. They developed a powerful kingdom in Great Zimbabwe. However, as with Mapungubwe, Zimbabwe's centralized political power structure was unarguably connected to the elites' capacity to control rain-making ritual powers, make connections with coastal states, and extensive investments in cattle rearing.

Excavations at the site of Great Zimbabwe unearthed an architectural edifice in the form of a huge stone that served as a royal centre of a large pre-colonial settlement. The royal centre was divided into two sprawling sections, hill and valley, each comprising a maze of stone enclosures, the importance of which is still being debated among scholars. While some scholars suggested that these monuments showed male/female structural dichotomy observed in Shona traditions, others claim that each enclosure was built individually and later abandoned with time. Recent findings suggested that the structures were built for shifting rulers' palaces from hilltop to valley, indicating a gradual shift in the primary sources of political authority, possibly toward bureaucratic and non-ritual modes, over time.

Additionally, regional patterns of state evolution in sub-Saharan Africa suggested that Great Zimbabwe was organized along hierarchical lines similar to its neighbours. The Zimbabwe sites marked by the storage of agricultural surpluses and barrow burials, potentially for local chiefs, are well distributed across the plateau. The systematic distribution of these sites reflects the fact that Great Zimbabwe, just like other indigenous states of its kind, was at the apex of a multi-layered settlement hierarchy indicating political centralization.

Precolonial Leadership Structures in Sub-Sahara Africa: Selected Cases

1. The Oyo Empire (1400 - 1835)

The Oyo Empire was a pre-colonial state in Western Nigeria, and it developed a highly organized political structure to govern its vast territorial domains.

The Alaafin of Oyo

The Alaafin of Oyo (owner of the Oyo palace) was the supreme head of the Oyo Empire. He was responsible for settling internal disputes among sub-rulers, keeping the tributaries safe from external attacks, and mediating between the chiefs and their people. The Alaafin was also expected to honour his worthy subordinates and subjects with chieftaincy titles. In return, all village heads had to pay homage to the king and renew their allegiance annually in specially organized ceremonies. The most important of these royal ceremonies are the Bere Festival, which is held to celebrate the king's reign and giant strides in governance. The Bere Festival was also meant to usher in a period of peace and stability across the empire for the next three years.

The Alaafin could be compelled to commit ritual suicide if the people lose confidence in him. This was done by sending the Bashorun to present him with either a dish of parrot's eggs or an empty calabash to pass a message of rejection. According to tradition, the Oba was expected to commit suicide thereafter. No Alaafin had ever rejected the people's verdict in history.

Leadership Succession in Oyo Empire

Oyo Empire was not a purely absolute monarchy, nor was it a hereditary one. The privy council of the Oyo Mesi chose the Alaafin from the descendants of Oranmiyan (the founder of Oyo). However, the new king might not be closely related to his immediate predecessor. In earlier times, the Alaafin's eldest son would succeed his late father. This arrangement encouraged the so-called Aremo (heir apparent) to hasten the death of his father. To prevent this ugly occurrence, it became a state policy for the crown prince to be forced to commit ritual suicide upon his father's demise. Howbeit, the crown prince, was quite powerful in his own right. For instance, the Alaafin could not leave his palace by tradition, except during important festivals, which in practice, limited his powers.

In contrast, the Aremo was free to supervise the day-to-day affairs of governance. This led the famous historian, Rev. Samuel Johnson, to declare: "The father is the king of the palace, and the son the king for the general public." In reality, the two traditional councils, Oyo Mesi and Ogboni, which checkmated the powers of Alaafin, tended to select a weak ruler immediately after the reign of a strong one to keep the throne from becoming too powerful.

The Councils

While the Alaafin was the supreme ruler of the empire, he did not rule without checks and balances on his powers. The Oyo Mesi and the Ogboni cult kept the king's powers in check. While the Oyo Mesi represented the political class, the Ogboni represented the people and were backed by native traditions. Thus, the power of the Alaafin in relation to these two councils, at any time, depended on his political shrewdness, sagacity, and personality traits.

The Ilari

The Alaafin appointed some government and religious officials, who were eunuchs known as the Ilari or half-heads (because of the custom of shaving off half of their hair); these state officials were evenly divided between both sexes. The senior Ilaris acted as palace guards or served as messengers sent to bear sacrifices to the other world, while the junior Ilaris undertook menial tasks. They bore titles such as Madarikan ("do not oppose") or Oba l'olu ("the oba is supreme"). Sub-courts of the Oyo Empire had Ilaris, who served as tax collectors and spies reporting to the Alaafin-in-council. The king would sometimes appoint these officials to visit and reside in tributary states such as Dahomey, Egbado, and Igbomina areas and to collect state taxes, as well as report on successes in military exploits so their king could get a share of the booties.

The Eso Military Class

Oyo Empire had a semi-professional army made up of specialist cavalry soldiers referred to as the Eso of Ikoyi. It is made up of 70 senior military war chiefs nominated by the Oyo Mesi and appointed by the Alaafin himself. The Eso were selected for their professionalism and military skills with no regard to their lineage, although de facto dynasties of the Eso also existed. The Eso was led by a generalissimo called the Are-Ona-Kakanfo (Field Marshal) and was noted for living by a code of war similar to the Japanese Samurai. A lot has been written about the high degree of professionalism in the ranks of Oyo military officers. Its notable military successes were attributable to its cavalry and the leadership of the officer cadre. There is no doubt that this professional approach contributed to so many victories recorded by Oyo military Generals.

2. The Benin Empire (1180 - 1897)

The Benin Empire was also a pre-colonial state situated in present-day southern Nigeria. Benin was one of the most highly organized empires in the coastal hinterland of Africa. It emerged around the 12th century CE from an ancient kingdom hitherto ruled by the Ogisos, called "lords of the sky." The first Oba (king) of Benin was Eweka I, the son of Oranmiyan, founder of Oyo, and heir to the Oduduwa throne at Ile-Ife. Thus, Eweka is the originator of a new dynasty in Edo (Benin City), the capital centre, which explains the link between the Bini and Yoruba ruling houses.

The Divinity of the Oba

In the Benin Empire, the Oba was regarded as a divine being. The Oba's sacredness was the centrepiece of his kingship. He was shrouded in a great mystery, and just like the Alaafin of Oyo, he could only leave his palace during important ceremonies or festivals. The Oba of Benin had the executive, legislature, and judiciary powers reposed in him, and he was also credited with magical powers. It was once punishable by death to say that the Oba performed human acts such as eating, bathing, sleeping, or dying.

Like their Yoruba neighbours, the Benin pre-colonial system of government was monarchical. The Oba was the supreme political leader in the Benin Empire with absolute authority. Unlike the Alaafin, however, the Oba was not bound by the laws of the land. Howbeit, the Oba was assisted in his administrative duties by royal councils and officials. The highest of such councils was the Uzama, made up of the Oliha (the most senior chief), Edohen, Ezomo, Ero, Eholo-nire, Oloton, and Edaiken (crown prince), who advised him on important matters of state.

As mentioned earlier, the Oba of Benin was not bound to the advice or decisions of his chiefs, unlike Yoruba kings. The Uzama were also responsible for crowning a new Oba (being the eldest surviving son of a preceding king). Benin had a primogeniture leadership succession plan in which the eldest son (Edaiken) would ascend the throne at the demise of his father.

Apart from the Uzama, many state officials assisted the king in administering the empire. These included officials like Eribo and Unwagwe, who were in charge of trade. Others were Ologbosere (the chief priest), Iyasere, and Ebohon, each having specific administrative roles in the empire.

Benin had two social classes: the nobles and the commoners. Administrative officials and traditional chiefs were mostly selected from the noble class. These included the Iwagwe who supplied the Oba's personal assistants, the Ibiwe who was in charge of the Oba's harem, and the Iwebo who took care of the Oba's regalia.

Culture and language were not strictly enforced in Benin Empire but localized within each subgroup of the empire. However, a representative (Enogie) was often appointed by the Oba to supervise specific areas.

The Military Class

A well-trained, disciplined army undertook military expeditions in Benin Empire. The head of the Benin army was the Oba of Benin, who served as the supreme military commander. Beneath the Oba were his subordinate generals, such as the Iyase, the Ezomo, and numerous others who supervised a Royal Regiment and served as palace guards and a Metropolitan Regiment based in the capital city. The queen mother or Iyoba Benin, also maintained her military regiment. Both the Royal and Metropolitan regiments could be regarded as relatively permanent formations. These were complemented by the Village Regiments, which were mobilized when needed and provided the bulk of the fighting force.

3. The Tiv People

The Tivs were stateless people found in the north-central and north-eastern parts of present-day Nigeria. Their pre-colonial societies were characterized by decentralized political authority assisted by sundry administrative and judicial institutions. A council of elders; maintained law and order in their political system at different levels of lineage.

The Tiv were a unique people belonging to the semi-Bantu linguistic family that spoke a common language and had peculiar religious practices and political ideologies. In the precolonial era, the Tiv traditional political system had no single leader wielding political power. Each Tiv belonged to several segments in lineage, with the "ITYO" as the smallest. In this setting, the Tiv enjoyed political citizenship, the right to life, and other rights. They lived in a cluster of huts known as the "YA" (compound). Each "ITYO" operated by patrilineage, by which inheritance would be traced to the father.

The Ityo

The Ityo is of supreme importance in Tivland as no one could go beyond their ityo (hembe ityo ga). The structural unit provided both the political and social contexts with which the Tiv was regarded in society. The Ityo council or Ijir (judgement) had economic, political, and religious responsibilities, which they discharged according to local traditions. Its membership is comprised of different sub-lineages, including individual families and households. The Ityo council had sovereign responsibilities, and its decisions were binding on all members.

The Orya

In Tivland, while the household was the most important unit in their political system, the lineage was the most elaborate. Each Tiv recognized authority in the status of their social order. They had political objectives of "TAR SORUN" (land repair). In the process of repairing their land, councils of the "Orya" and "Ityo" were most important. Each "YA" was named after its Orya and administered by a council of elders.

The Kwav

The Kwav or age-grade associations were inaugurated every three years from within members of the same age group. From twenty and seventy years, there could be up to twenty Kwav. Members of the same Kwav could offer mutual help on their farms called ihyumbe, and they could also mobilize friends in defence against witchcraft. The support given to a member would depend on his wealth, generosity, and influence.

The Kur

The Kur was usually a brave warrior or hunter who possessed the qualities of a good fighter. The Tiv militia leader was the kur utya, the military chief, who led them in war. When a man aspired to become the Kur, he would lead the people in battle and defend them from external aggression.

4. The Akan People

The Akan were a meta-ethnic group of people predominantly speaking the Central Tano languages and located in what is now the southern regions of Ghana and the former Ivory Coast region. The Akans were the largest ethnic group in those states and had a significant presence in Benin, Burkina Faso, Guinea, Liberia, and Togo. The Akan people have dominated gold mining and trading in those places from the 15th century to the advent of colonialism in the 19th century.

Leadership Succession in the Akan Culture

The political system operated by the Akans allowed the Queen Mother to nominate a suitable candidate to replace a ruler who dies or abdicates the throne. She would present her choice to the Akan kingmakers, who would either accept or reject such nominees. In doing this, the Queen Mother was expected to consult the elders, members of the royal family, and other influential personalities to ascertain their wishes.

Moreover, the kingmakers could reject the Queen Mother's nominee, but she could continue nominating candidates until an acceptable candidate is found. Otherwise, the Council of Elders would choose a suitable person from the royal family.

The Akan Council of Elders

The Akan political system had a Council of Elders comprising the most senior Captains of Asafo Companies. It included the heads of the leading lineages and representatives of the various clans. In this regard, the ultimate political authority resided with the people but was held in trust by their representatives in the Council of Elders. Before important state policies were formulated and implemented, the Akans' paramount ruler had to consult with this council of Elders and his senior chiefs.

Oath of Office in Akan Culture

When installing a new chief, the Council of Elders would make the chief swear to an oath of allegiance to always abide by the norms and traditions of the land. He would also be advised to see the importance of consulting with the elders before making any important decision.

Destoolment of Akan Chief

An Akan chief could easily lose his authority if he disobeyed the advice of the elders if he was unable to maintain the stool property or protect his people.

Administration of Justice in Akan

The Akan Council of Elders used arbitration, mediation, and conciliation in settling disputes among the people. Each disputant would be given a fair trial. For instance, complainants and the accused would be allowed to argue their cases and be cross-examined by the Council. After deliberating over the case, the elders would then pass their judgement. It is also important to note that the commoners have considerable power in the Akan political system. They could agitate against their chief if they lose confidence in his leadership ability.

5. Lozi People

The Lozi or Barotse was a large group of autonomous kingdoms of more than 46 different ethnic groups found in what is now known as western Zambia. The Lozi were also referred to as the Malozi,

Makololo, Nyambe, Barotse, Rozi, or Rotse. Lozi tradition claims that they had inhabited Barotseland from time immemorial.

The Political System of the Lozis

The political organization of the Barotse was centred on the monarch whose head or Paramount Ruler was known as "Litunga," - keeper of the earth. The Lozi society was highly stratified, with the Litunga at the top and members of the royal family occupying prominent positions in society. The Barotse royal establishment was known as Mulonga, and the Lozi tolerated little or no criticism of even an unpopular Litunga. Unlike other African ethnic groups, the Lozi belonged to a single culture and never separated into different clans. The precolonial history of the Lozi has a long line of female rulers before Mwanasolundwi Muyunda, the son of Mbuymamwambwa, established the current patrilineal system of leadership succession. A new Litunga must come from the line of kings, preferably a son of a former Litunga, born after his father accedes to the throne, by a mother on whom royal titles have been bestowed.

The Litunga was assisted in administering the land by the Moyo (principal consort), the Mulena (heir apparent), Mulena Mukwai (royal princess), Mwana Mulena (prince), Mukwai (princess), and Makoshi (Litunga's official sister).

Learning from the Past: Important Lessons from Pre-Colonial Governance in Sub-Saharan Africa

While much attention has been focused on building good leadership and governance institutions in SSA modelled on foreign leadership concepts, less attention has been paid to how Africa's past can provide suitable lessons on leadership and how its precolonial leaders can serve as good role models for today's African leaders. The neglect of Africa's past leadership achievements and its lessons to modern Africa is understandable, given that much of the development and governance thinking has been dominated by Western ideas.

Much of the knowledge about Africa has been produced by Non-Africans, and where Africans have tried to write about Africa from the perspectives of Africans, this has been dismissed as nationalist historiography worth nothing more than a cursory glance. There have been deliberate efforts to persuade Africans to forget their past and focus entirely on the present and future trajectories as if Africa's development can be disconnected from its history. Even when lessons are drawn from Africa's pre-colonial leadership styles, these tend to be seen as only suitable to past conditions with no relevance whatsoever to the complex challenges of the 21st Century.

Although there may be some truth to the argument, such views risk presenting a simplistic version of the complex circumstances under which pre-colonial leadership and governance systems evolved. Similarly, such ideas will end up with wrong conclusions as if there is nothing significant present leaders can learn from pre-colonial leadership and governance systems. Besides, the phenomenon of effective leadership is enduring and can never be restricted to a particular political epoch, no matter how plausible this may seem.

Hence, this research contends that there are numerous lessons current African leaders can learn from the past in resolving the present challenges confronting the continent. It is also argued that instead of looking to the West or East for leadership recipes, the leaders should dig into Africa's past leadership successes and challenges, build on these in combination with other relevant recipes for them to create unique and workable solutions to resolve problems facing their people.

Pre-colonial Africa is replete with various examples of successful and influential leaders who built great empires and kingdoms, albeit not without challenges. These leaders showcased a high level of strategic thinking, allowing them to take advantage of existing opportunities for their societal development. Some of the valuable lessons to learn from these past leadership constructs in SSA include:

1.   Promotion of both interregional and intraregional trade;

2.   Diversification of the economy by promoting other economic activities including crop cultivation, livestock keeping, fishing, metalworking (iron and gold), and cotton weaving;

3.   Introduction of democratic systems of government; and

4.   Acquiring relevant knowledge from outside.

To start with, the importance of economic diversification cannot be overemphasized. Although the economies of the empires and kingdoms of Africa were based mainly on trade, several other economic activities were undertaken and encouraged, thus guaranteeing economic prosperity to the people. For example, in the Songhai Empire, apart from trade, other economic activities that were undertaken include farming, craft making, and fishing. Moreover, the Mali Empire has prospered and avoided famine that beset Ghana mainly because it encouraged expanded food production, animal keeping, fishing, metal works, woodworks, and trade. All these made the empires grow economically as it became possible for them to feed themselves and gather a range of commodities for exchange.

Nowadays, almost all African economies are characterized by heavy dependence on one sector or two. Nigeria, for instance, has been heavily dependent on its oil since the 1970s to the detriment of its once buoyant agricultural sector.

Similarly, Angola's economy has been heavily dependent on oil production because all other sectors of its economy have been neglected, leaving the country to be over-reliant on oil revenues to finance imports. Therefore, it is significant for African countries to look back into history and learn from precolonial economies to diversify their economies away from over-dependence on natural resources over which they have little or no control on the international prices.

In 2017, the World Economic Forum (WEF) ranked Nigeria (the largest economy in Africa) 125 out of 137 countries in its Global Competitiveness Report. The WEF Survey found that Nigeria's potential for structural change was impeded by inadequate investment in infrastructure, technology, higher education, and innovation. As stated above, Nigeria has long depended on crude oil as its economic mainstay, with feeble attempts aimed at diversification over the years. A recent Bloomberg report finds that this one-source revenue base is unsustainable.

Secondly, collecting revenues and proper use of collected revenues remains one of the major challenges confronting countries in Sub-Saharan Africa. Revenue collection is very important since no government can perform its statutory roles without adequate revenues. This is probably why precolonial African states never joked with revenue collection. For example, in the old Ghana Empire, the king collected tax from all traders in Ghana and used the revenues to finance governmental activities.

In contrast, existing African states have continued to struggle with collecting and using revenues to some extent. Revenue collection in these countries is hampered by widespread tax evasion and tax avoidance by citizens, corporations, and even the wealthy elites. Contrary to what was obtained in precolonial states like Ghana and Mali, where no foreigner was exempted from paying taxes, African countries have not been taxing all people and corporations due to generous tax incentives designed to woo foreign investors. For example, it has been reported that the four East African countries of Kenya, Rwanda, Tanzania and Uganda, are losing not less than $5 billion annually from tax incentives and exemptions granted to some corporations. In Nigeria, the erstwhile Coordinating Minister of the Economy, Dr Ngozi Okonjo-Iweala, disclosed in 2014 that as many as 65 per cent of companies in Nigeria had declined to forward their tax returns, and a whopping 75 per cent of the eligible taxpayers were not in the Federal Inland Revenue Service (FIRS) tax net.

Unless African leaders take tax/revenue collection and spending seriously, there can be no assurance that development challenges will be overcome.

Thirdly, there is a need to borrow knowledge and expertise from outside. In the 21st Century, we have seen a shift towards the knowledge-based economy in which skills and expertise are more prized than crude resources. In this digital age, countries with little or no expertise in certain fields can easily learn, borrow, or adapt from where these are readily available. Some countries even go as far as carrying out cyber espionage on other countries as a way of acquiring the desired knowledge and expertise with which to achieve one technological breakthrough or the other. This is what the leaders of the ancient Mali Empire did to put Mali on the world map. After attending his pilgrimage in the Holy Land, Mansa Musa brought many Muslim scholars, artists, scientists, and architects back with him to Mali and made use of their knowledge in building a strong empire. He similarly encouraged the spread of Islamic education throughout his domain. Current African leaders should also embrace the acquisition of knowledge and expertise from other places and use the skills gained to develop their countries.

Furthermore, one of Africa's major economic challenges in the 21st Century is that there is little intra-African trade. Much of the trade relations in Africa is between African countries and the West or Asia. From 1997 to 2011 alone, the intra-African trade share declined from 22.4 per cent to about 12 per cent. It is argued that trading within Africa is costlier than trading with the outside world, given the fact that many African countries are bedevilled with poor infrastructure, unfriendly tariffs, and corrupt government officials. For so long, Africans have been urged to develop strong inter-trade ties as a means of shielding themselves from the vagaries of the global commodity markets, though this is yet to be heeded to.

Looking back into history, precolonial African societies appear to have involved themselves in considerable intraregional trade long before trading with the external world. For example, when the Portuguese arrived in West Africa in 1471, they found that the people of Benin and Ghana were already trading with neighbouring societies.

Equally important is the fact that these pre-colonial African leaders were not autocratic. There were genuine democratic elements in traditional African societies, which could somehow be related to present-day democratic ideals. Although the emperors or kings wielded enormous powers, such powers were usually balanced and checked as citizens were, directly and indirectly, involved in the daily activities of governance. Precolonial African leaders were also duty-bound to observe local customs and traditions, failing which they would be deposed or asked to abdicate the throne.

Important to modern Africa is the need to create strong governance and leadership institutions that can outlive leaders' lifespan or tenure. This is very important because many African countries lack coherent and strong institutions to withstand any internal or external challenges. The ancient African empires expanded mainly because they had viable governance systems and strong leaders who could expand and protect them economically and territorially. Suffice it to say that most of these early states collapsed after the demise of strong leaders or by conquests. Current African leaders need to see this as a challenge and an opportunity to create long-lasting leadership institutions that can outlive them.

Conclusion

It has been scientifically established that Africa is the cradle of civilization and that the human race also originated from the continent. Many societies in SSA had comparatively advanced institutions even before making contact with Europeans in the 15th Century. These foreigners were surprised by the sophisticated political structures they found in Songhai, Mali, Ghana, Benin, Oyo, Zimbabwe, and other indigenous African kingdoms and empires. For instance, the British explorers Richard Lander and Hugh Clapperton, who visited Badagry on the West African coast in the early 19th Century, commended the safety, law, and order of the Oyo Empire under the Alaafin. Also, Ibn Battuta, the famous Islamic scholar who visited Mali Empire in the mid-14th Century, acknowledged the Empire's good administration, security, lack of oppression, and conflict resolution system. Similarly, a Dutchman who visited the Benin Empire in the 1600s described its capital (Edo) as far more civilized than many European cities of the era.

In commerce, there is enough archaeological evidence to show that African societies knew much about cloth making, mining, farming, metal fabrication, gold, and silversmith, as well as food production. From the available literature, we have also learned that local manufacturers in pre-colonial Africa were creating products of comparable and, in many instances, even of higher quality than those from pre-industrial Europe. Benin Bronze works were found to be of high quality and beauty compared to those produced in other parts of the world.

Also, pre-colonial African history has shown that pre-colonial African societies had advanced leadership institutions, which were organic products of social evolution over centuries. They had their kings and chiefs, most of whom were accountable to the people through their representatives. For instance, the Oyo Empire had established a democratic system with checks and balances maintained by the Oyo Mesi and the Ogboni, who could discipline any erring Alaafin. This was around the time that England, France, and Germany were still grappling with the excesses of their emperors and kings. Oyo monarchs never had absolute powers like their contemporary European rulers, such as Napoleon Bonaparte of France, Frederick William of Prussia, and Louis XIV of France, who was said to have proclaimed, "I am the state!"

Additionally, SSA's past is also replete with stories of influential and successful rulers or leaders such as Ewuare of the Great of Benin

Empire, Yekuno Amlak, and Oranmiyan Mansa Musa of Mali, who built great kingdoms and empires and maintained them, although not without challenges. There were also some examples of leaders who built their states through trade and farming and proceeds from the notorious trans-Atlantic slave trade. Whatever the case, those leadership achievements signified a high level of thinking and planning, which allowed them to take advantage of opportunities for their societal development.

Going by the various African cultures discussed earlier, one finds that there are important lessons that current African leaders can learn from the rulers of the past. One is that decision by consensus was often the order in African deliberations and was so in principle. Democratic norms, including consultation, accountability, choice, and freedom of expression, were prevalent in traditional African societies. It is also pertinent to note that the community's active participation in its political affairs was the hallmark of indigenous African societies and cultures. Besides, holding political office in pre-colonial Africa did not attract any form of special remuneration. However, the people often appreciate their leaders with gifts and surpluses from their farm harvests. This contrasts with the outrageous monetary benefits and allowances attached to modern political offices in Africa, which have made them too attractive to warrant electoral violence and cutthroat competition among the political class. Except on a few occasions, the people often took the outcome of leadership selection or election processes in indigenous African societies with equanimity since Africans believed that it was an act of God.

So far, this chapter has tried to tell the stories of SSA's past and highlight their leadership practices for the present crop of African leaders to emulate and learn from. However, it can be argued that such governance systems only suited the material conditions of the past. However, much of what the leaders did is still relevant today. Such issues as democratic governance, revenue collection, consultation, consensus building, decision making, leadership succession, skills acquisition, military campaigns, and trade are still very important in modern business and public administration.

4

STRUCTURE OF COLONIAL INFILTRATION IN AFRICA

Chapter 4

The European colonization of sub-Saharan Africa was a monumental milestone in the history of the region. Many Africans see the impact of colonization to possibly be the most significant factor in understanding the present conditions of African life. Thus, thorough scrutiny of the phenomenon known as colonialism is required to appreciate the extent to which it affected the socio-political development of Africa and Africans, as well as the way they perceive themselves.

Hence, this chapter focuses on the incursion of colonialism into Africa and its leadership systems. As in the previous chapter, the resulting events will be discussed on a sub-regional basis, beginning with West Africa and then East and Southern Africa.

The Spectacle of Colonial Incursion into Africa

Europe's two largest colonial powers in Africa were Britain and France, both of which controlled about 70 per cent of the region before WWI and more than 80 per cent after that. The period between the mid-1800s and the early 1900s marked the zenith of colonial hold on Africa. The imperial rule in Africa was formalized at the Berlin Conference, which was held from 1884 to 1885 in the German city of Berlin. At that conference, all the European colonial powers met and partitioned Africa, and recognizing each other's sphere of influence or control of different parts of the continent of Africa. The conference was convened to reach an agreement on the colonially created boundaries as a way of avoiding conflicts between and among European powers such as Britain, France, Germany, Italy, Belgium, Portugal, and Spain. Following her defeat in WWI, Germany was stripped of her former colonies, which were shared out to the victorious parties held as trusteeships under the League of Nations' mandate. The German East African territories of Burundi and Rwanda went to Belgium, while Tanganyika (mainland part of Tanzania) went to Britain. Togoland went to France, but a small stripe of land along its western border became a British trust, governed with the Gold Coast (Ghana). Kamerun (Cameroon) was split into two; the southwestern portion became a British trust, while the rest went to France. Also, South West Africa (Namibia) was assigned to South Africa as compensation for the country fighting alongside the Allied Powers in the Great War.

At this junction, readers may be interested in knowing what attracted the European powers to Africa in the first place. One researcher of Portuguese imperial history stated that the Portuguese explorers were moved by, in his words, "a crusading zeal, the desire for Guinea gold, the quest for [the mythical Christian kingdom of] Prester John, and the search for spices."

We may also consider Ali Mazrui's three reasons for European incursion into Africa, which subsequently led to colonization. The first reason stemmed from European ethnocentrism rooted in Western Christian belief. The Christian doctrines (and Islamic ones) implicitly implore believers to spread the gospel among unbelievers and win converts. Since most African people were seen as unbelievers, Europeans saw the opportunity to proselytize them. We should also not forget that the early years of both Christianity and Islam in Africa were characterized by evangelical missions working alongside military conquests, which were aimed at grabbing the land. Other methods of persuasion were later introduced when various missionary societies dispatched missionaries to establish missions, build schools, hospitals, and other social service centres in a bid to disseminate Christian doctrines across Africa. For instance, David Livingstone, David Hinderer, Mary Slessor, Thomas Birch Freeman, and others were able to combine church missionary activities with humanitarian services in Africa as part of their soul-winning efforts.

The second reason was somewhat based on imperialism and the desire by various European patriots to contribute to their country's claim to grandeur by gaining colonies abroad. Britain's Cecil Rhodes secured a huge chunk of Central and East Africa for the British Crown. Karl Peters' exploits opened the way for Germany's imperial claim to Tanganyika. Sir George Goldie secured about two-thirds of Nigeria for Britain through his Royal Niger Company. Morton

Stanley's expeditions opened the way for the Belgian King, King Leopold, to acquire Congo.

The third reason has a lot to do with gathering scientific knowledge about the unknown world. Subsequently, Africa, often referred to as the 'Dark Continent,' aptly provided the right kind of challenge to the European scientific community. It held so much mystery for the foreign explorers, who travelled through the African hinterland and recorded all they saw. For this reason, the majority of the early explorers of Africa were geographers who were fascinated by the exotic qualities of the land. Expeditions led by people like John Speke, Joseph Thompson, Richard Burton, Samuel Baker, and others in the 19th century, planned in the name of science and discovery, served to attract the interest of the wider European scientific community to Africa. They explored rivers and mountains, waterfalls, and mining sites, and they also studied local cultures and recorded the experiences in their logbooks. Their records eventually promoted the interest of other Europeans in Africa.

Of course, the three reasons outlined above are not mutually exclusive; but somehow interrelated. For instance, scientific information provided by the early explorers was often collected and evaluated by European governments to decide if particular areas were worth being colonized. If the information supplied suggested that an area had friendly people, a pleasant climate, or evidence of natural resources, the government would sponsor an expeditionary force to control the land. Often, the initial exploratory trips were subsidized or funded by European governments or government-chartered organizations such as the Royal Geographical Society. In some cases, the explorers could not resist the temptation of amassing wealth for themselves by pillaging African villages. In situations where the explorers or missionaries encountered local hostility, foreign troops were usually mobilized to appease the groups involved or to protect the foreigners. Such was the case of Bishop Hannington, who was murdered for his religious activities in Uganda on the orders of a local king, which prompted the eventual colonization of the land by Britain.

Further, the colonial rule also saw a close working relationship between the colonial authorities and the missionaries. In colonial Africa, schools were established and staffed by church missionaries but subsidized by colonial governments, whose primary interest in missionary education for Africans was to meet the human resource needs of colonial bureaucracies.

Mission schools taught that the Europeans were in Africa to civilize the barbarians, and missionaries had complete control over the schools' curriculum. African culture, heritage, and traditions were ridiculed and suppressed in missionary schools, while European languages were greatly encouraged. The goal was to give Africans a different identity by compelling them to use Christian names, a practice still in vogue till today. In many ways, Christianity instilled the spirit of submissiveness in Africans by stressing that life was transient and should be used for preparing for eternal life in the coming heavenly kingdom. To qualify for this eternal life, Africans were taught to imbibe Christian virtues of humility, patience, and submissiveness to authority. Thus, humiliation and suffering, a common feature of colonial rule, were said to be ennobling. Gradually, Africans began to surrender the fundamental elements of their traditional belief system.

Besides, missionary work was not limited to spiritual matters of spreading the gospel of Jesus. A common saying in Africa, attributed to Jomo Kenyatta (Kenya's first president), carries some truth about this. It goes like this: "When Europeans first came to Africa, they had the Bible, and Africans owned the land. They gave us the Bible and told us to close our eyes in prayer. When we opened our eyes, the Europeans had our land. In contrast, we have their Bible." This assertion reflected the Congolese experience, in particular, where the missions undertook the task to civilize Africans and turn them into "black Europeans."

From the foregoing, we can see why several social scientists and writers have appraised the role of church missionaries in Africa as having aided colonial oppression.

Having read how Europeans came into Africa on the heels of explorers and missionaries, one may wonder why those foreigners were so keen to acquire colonies in the region. Three reasons could be categorized as follows: economic, cultural, and political/strategic. To start with, the economic reasons for colonization have received the greatest attention from scholars. Early literature on African colonization contained ample references to Africa's vast resources, the market potential represented by the region, and the economic benefits that would accrue to the colonialists by exploring the places. The economic rationale for colonizing the Third World was systematically articulated by V.I. Lenin in his classic "Imperialism: The Highest State of Capitalism." Lenin argued that European powers sought colonies in Africa in response to their capitalist economies' inherent demands, which required enormous natural resources for their industries and to exploit the plentiful cheap labour in Africa. Also, as the European economies expanded, Third World colonies became increasingly necessary for disposing of surplus goods and making huge profits. Suffice it to say that the overarching desire for wealth, resources, cheap labour, and trade was a major motivation for European incursion into Africa.

The cultural motivation for African colonization is rooted in Europeans' ethnocentric attitude, which saw anyone of a different race as culturally inferior, be it African or Asian. In the particular case of Africans, because their historical achievements were not documented and unknown to the outside world, the colonialists felt it was their divine duty to civilize the African "savages." Once the decision to colonize Africa had been made, it was subsequently left to European intellectuals, poets, and writers to provide the philosophical and moral justifications for colonialism. This task was undertaken by people like Rudyard Kipling (whose racist poem was quoted at the beginning of this chapter), Joseph Conrad in his book: The Heart of Darkness, and others who sought to justify colonialism through their works.

Lastly, the political reason for colonization was competition among European powers for dominance in the prevalent international system of the 18th to 19th centuries. Those nations saw colonial possessions as a source of international prestige and influence. Even today, one can still argue that such possessions bestow special status on those who have them. So, powerful countries did compete with each other for influence in smaller countries. The Cold War between the Soviet Union and the United States rested largely on the competition for dominance in world affairs. Such international interventions in history played out in Vietnam (by the US), Afghanistan (by the USSR and later by the US), Iraq (by the US), Syria (by Iran, Russia, and the US), and Yemen (by a coalition led by Saudi Arabia and the UAE), and this has been described as attempts at projecting power and hoping to bring the respective countries into their spheres of influence.

Let us now examine the African colonial experience on a regional basis as promised.

The Colonial Incursion into West Africa

The scramble for Africa among European powers culminated in the Berlin Conference called by the German Chancellor Otto von Bismarck to partition Africa on amicable terms. The conference settled issues of freedom of navigation along the Congo and Niger rivers and other claims to African coasts. In retrospect, the story of colonialism in West Africa after this conference revolved around five major themes, namely: the establishment of European colonies, the development of those colonies through forced labour, the consolidation of colonial authority, the transformation of West Africa along cultural and socio-political lines, as well as eventual resistance to colonial administration by the people.

A clause in the Berlin Treaty of 1885 explicitly gave European powers the right to use military force to occupy West African territories. This authority was enforced between 1885 and 1914 when the Europeans established European protectorates across West Africa from Calabar to Dakar. The protectorates were mere stop-gaps before the eventual occupation of West Africa. Africans naturally rejected both the protectorates and the subsequent occupation by adopting strategies such as diplomacy, forming alliances, and engaging in an outright military confrontation. Some of these strategies shall be addressed below.

African Diplomatic Attempts at Forestalling European Occupation

In their quest to build a West African colonial empire, Britain found the Ashanti people of Ghana the most difficult to subdue. For example, the Ashanti wars against the British colonialists lasted for a whole hundred years, beginning from 1805 with casualties on both sides. At the same time, numerous diplomatic attempts were made by the Ashanti to curtail British incursion into their land, failing which military confrontations ensued.

Along the same line, King Moro Nabaor of the Mossi told French Captain, Restenave in 1895 that:

"I know the whites wish to kill me to take my country, and yet you claim that they will help me to organize my country. But I find my country good just as it is. I do not need them. I know what is necessary for me and what I want. I have my merchants: consider yourself fortunate that I do not order your head to be cut off. Go away now, and above all, never come back."

Moreover, whenever West African kings struck alliances with the European colonialists, they intended to enhance their diplomatic advantage. For instance, King Jaja of Opobo (in what is now known as southern Nigeria) resorted to diplomacy to resist European imperialism. Historical records showed that Jubo Jubogha or Mbanaso Ozurumba, a.k.a Jaja of Opobo, was a former slave of Igbo origin. The Anna Pepple House of Bonny, Nigeria, elected him king in 1863 following the death of his master. A power struggle later ensued between the Anna Pepple House and the neighbouring Manilla Pepple House of Bonny, which led to the outbreak of a civil war in 1869. This prompted King Jaja to migrate elsewhere to establish an inland kingdom at Opobo, in the oil-palm-producing hinterland.

As an avowed nationalist, Jaja was determined to control oil trades in his domain and prevent Europeans from interfering with the proceeds. The king entered into a diplomatic alliance by signing a trade agreement with British officials in 1873. This treaty acknowledged Jaja as the ruler of Opobo and the foremost middleman on the lower Niger River. The scramble for Africa among European powers later in the century would upset the understanding with various consequences.

In the aftermath, British officials and merchants ceased to honour the terms of the treaty. They started making incursions into the interior to open up trade while sidelining such African middlemen as Jaja and King Nana of Itsekiri. In this atmosphere, confrontations became inevitable. This turn of events culminated in the 1887 invitation to King Jaja by the British consul, Harry Johnson, requesting Jaja to board a British gunboat for discussions and with no foreknowledge of the devious British plans, he honoured the invitation, and that was the last time he set foot on Opobo soil. He was exiled to the West Indies and then to Tenerife, Spain, where he died in 1891.

Military Confrontations with the Imperialists

The European imperialists did not find it easy colonizing West African states. The history of the period 1880-1914 is replete with military clashes between African militiamen and the well-oiled machinery of British regiments. The Ashanti, Benin Empire, Ijebu Kingdom, Sokoto Caliphate, Dahomey Kingdom, and the city of Lagos once faced bombardments from British naval forces. Some decentralized African societies equally resisted the imperialist intentions. The Baule of Ivory Coast, the Tiv, and the Igbo of Nigeria offered stiff resistance to colonialism. The Tiv fought the British colonialists from 1900 to 1930. The Baule fought French forces from 1891 to 1911, while the Igbo resistance to British occupation was particularly prolonged. British officials found it very difficult to subjugate the Igbos because of the republican nature of their society, with no Igbo kings to co-opt into the indirect rule system. Therefore, the colonialists had to fight their way from one Igbo village to another before victory could be declared over the people. An Igbo Council of Elders once challenged British occupation of their land and told the British to ".......come and fight: if you want war, come, we are ready." The Igbos and the British fought numerous wars from 1898 to 1910.

Colonial Infiltration into East and Southern Africa

East Africa is the eastern portion of sub-Saharan Africa, comprising up to 20 countries, former colonial territories in the real sense, except Ethiopia. However, due to the colonial legacies of the British East Africa Protectorate and German East Africa colony, the term "East Africa" is often more closely associated with the areas now comprising the three countries of Kenya, Tanzania, and Uganda.

Portuguese explorers were the first European travellers to arrive in present-day Kenya and Tanzania by sea. Vasco da Gama first came to Mombasa in 1498. He succeeded in reaching India from there, a trip that enabled the Portuguese to establish a route to the Far East directly by the sea instead of the time-consuming land-sea route through the Persian Gulf. After the closure of land routes to India by the Ottoman Turks, the Portuguese hoped to use the newly discovered route to break the Venetian monopoly on the spices trade in Europe.

The initial Portuguese presence in the African Great Lakes region was focused on maintaining a shipping outpost centred on Mombasa, aimed at resupplying their ships and ocean-going vessels. The Portuguese occupation of the area officially began after 1505, when their flagship under Don Francisco de Almeida conquered Kilwa in southern Tanzania. This event was followed rapidly by more conquests made in Mombasa, Hoja (present-day Ungwana), Barawa, Angoche, Pate, and other coastal towns. The Portuguese forces; built forts and took measures to secure their domination of the region. Still, this dominance was cut short in the face of the British, Dutch, and Omani Arab infiltrations into the Great Lakes region in the 17th century.

The Omani Arabs constituted the greatest threat to Portuguese influence in the Great Lakes region. They ambushed Portuguese forces, attacked their naval forces, and finally sent them packing from Kenya and Tanzania's coasts by 1730. The Portuguese were then forced to retreat south to Portuguese East Africa (Mozambique), where they remained as colonial overlords until the 1975 independence of Mozambique.

Arab domination of the major ports on the Swahili coast of East Africa continued until it aroused British interests to end the slave trade in those places. By the late 19th century, the slave trade had been completely outlawed, and this was enforced by British naval forces that patrolled oceans and seas to inspect trading ships for slave cargo. This left the Omani Arabs little room to manoeuvre, and they were later expelled from Kenya ports by the Germans and British officials. Still, their presence continued to be felt in Zanzibar and Pemba until the 1964 Zanzibar Revolution that completely sent them packing from Africa.

Between the mid-19th and 20th centuries, eastern Africa became a centre of intense competition between various European powers of that time. In the scramble for Africa, almost every country in the region became part of a colonial empire to varying degrees. Mozambique came under Portuguese rule; Kenya, Mauritius (formerly under France), Seychelles, Tanzania, and Uganda under Britain; The Comoros, Djibouti, and Réunion under France; German East Africa (Burundi, Rwanda, and Tanganyika or mainland Tanzania); and finally, Eritrea and Somaliland under Italy.

From bases in Eritrea and Somaliland, the Italians launched the first Italo-Ethiopia War against Ethiopia in 1895. By 1896, the war had become a disaster for Italy, and Ethiopia retained its independence. However, the Italians launched another aggression in 1936, and this time, Ethiopia became part of Italian East Africa after its defeat. The Italian occupation of Ethiopia was rather short, and by 1941, the country regained its independence during WWII as part of the East African campaign.

Colonial infiltration into southern Africa was similar to the East African experience. By the middle of the 19th century, southern Africa was an area characterized by intense clashes between local militiamen and European settlers. The scale of these conflicts had increased throughout the 18th and early 19th centuries, resulting in significant demographic shifts among the African population. To understand why; it is necessary to trace the history to the early colonial period briefly.

By 1600 CE, two Bantu-speaking groups had established themselves in present-day South Africa. The Sotho-Tswana settled in the eastern highlands' region, while the Nguni settled across the eastern coastal belt. Both groups sought out fertile soils and reliable rainfall to sustain their pastoral agriculture. In addition to pastoralism, their subsistence economic activities included hunting and bartering. Human settlement patterns in southern Africa during the precolonial era thus reflected the climatic conditions of the area. The western half was much drier, while the eastern half had a high summer rainfall. The southwestern Cape had a Mediterranean climate with dry summers and wet winters. The southwestern cape area was also free of malaria parasites and tsetse fly.

The quality of the climate in the southwestern Cape was not entirely lost on European explorers who sailed around the southern tip of Africa on their way to India. First accomplished by the Portuguese, the Cape of Good Hope route attracted more Europeans to the region by the mid-16th century. The Vereenigde Oost-Indische Compagnie (VOC) or the Dutch East India Company was the first Europeans to settle down at Table Bay. They built a fort and a small trading port at the site in 1652, which served as Cape Town's beginnings as a modern city. Initially, VOC did not intend to colonize the area but focused on resupplying ships passing by with fresh stocks. With time, this trading post grew rapidly, and with it, the demand for labour. This trend necessitated the importation of slaves into Cape Town in 1658. The slaves were an eclectic mix coming from different places such as the Ceylon, Malay Peninsula, Madagascar, Java, and East Africa.

At first, VOC peacefully traded with the indigenous Khoekhoe population for herds of cattle and sheep. However, as more European stock farmers, known as Boers, advanced into the interior, more conflict with local people over land ensued. European incursion into the north and east of Cape Town grew steadily in the 17th and 18th centuries, despite concerted African resistance. Subsequently, the loss of land and the introduction of European diseases like smallpox resulted in the gradual disintegration of indigenous socio-political structures in southern Africa.

The San people of southern Africa were particularly treated with contempt by the Boers over what they described as their uncivilized lifestyle. Conflicts along the north-eastern frontier soon culminated in a genocidal campaign against the San between 1770 and 1780.

For the Boers, the most fertile land in South Africa laid to the east of Cape Town. This place also appealed to the Xhosa people, the southernmost Bantu-speaking pastoralists in Africa. Conflicts between the two ensued rapidly, and the two sides fought not less than nine wars from 1779 to 1879.

By 1795, the VOC faced bankruptcy. To prevent France from acquiring a foothold in the region, VOC facilitated the territory for Britain that same year. The British would introduce widespread social reforms to improve African labour conditions and restrict the power of European slave owners over their slaves or servants. These reforms were followed by the abolition of the slave trade in 1834 and then the founding of the Aborigines' Protection Society in 1837. As a result, the Boers were reprimanded for their treatment of Africans, raising their resentment against British rule at Cape Town.

The combination of labour reforms and the abolition of the slave trade resulted in the migration of Boers from the Cape Colony in large numbers into the southern African hinterland to escape British rule and to establish their cities. The migrations became commonly known as the Great Trek, and by the 1850s, the migrant Boers secured British recognition of their new republics of the Orange Free State and the Transvaal.

Table 3: Showing the adverse effect of the Slave Trade and Colonialism on African population in comparison with Europe an and Asian population from 1650-1900

Continent	Population (1650)	Population (1750)	Population (1850)	Population (1900)
Africa	100	100	100	120
Europe	103	144	274	423
Asia	257	437	656	857

Source: Walter Rodney – How Europe Underdeveloped Africa (Pg. 111)

Suffice it to say that these migrations into the African interior from the coast caused widespread socio-political upheavals among the indigenous Bantu-speaking people. The late 18th and early 19th centuries witnessed wars between the Africans and the Boers on one part and among the Nguni and Sotho-Tswana people on the other hand. These conflicts further resulted in waves of forced migrations and consolidation of colonial rule, later known as the "Mfecane" - the scattering. The ripple effect of the Mfecane would reach down to a vast geographical area in southern Africa, including South Africa, Lesotho, Malawi, Mozambique, Tanzania, Zambia, and Zimbabwe. It encouraged the rise of powerful African kingdoms such as the Ndebele under Mzilikazi, Zulu under Shaka, and Sotho under Moshoeshoe. As mentioned earlier, it also resulted in constant clashes between the Boers and the Ndebele and Zulu kingdoms, which characterized southern African life for the rest of the 19th century. Besides, it laid the foundation for the brutal Apartheid regime of the

Boers in South Africa, which took concerted efforts from the whole world before it was dismantled in the 1990s

Conclusion

A few key points stand out clearly in this chapter. Firstly, colonial infiltration into SSA was not a tea party. From Dakar to Benin to Cape Town, indigenous African people made arduous efforts, employing diplomacy and military confrontations, to prevent the intruders from accessing their land. But while the natives fought gallantly with crude weapons, the Europeans almost always won the battles with their superior firepower, and the rest is history.

Secondly, the reasons for the acquisition of colonies in Africa by the imperial powers included the need for raw materials for their industries, the search for new markets for their industrial products, the need to provide more food for Europe's growing urban population, and other selfish considerations. These reasons stand in contrast to the notion that the Europeans came into Africa to spread the gospel of Christ.

Thirdly, just like the trans-Atlantic Slave Trade, the colonization of Africa had adverse effects on Africa's population, leadership institutions, and governance system. Foremost, the partitioning of Africa at the Berlin Conference of 1884-1885 was done out of greed leading to the indiscriminate creation of territorial boundaries that ignored pre-existing ethnic boundaries and social cohesion, which had somehow kept indigenous African societies together. Europe's arbitrarily created borders in Africa remain to date a perpetual colonial liability that has not stopped to foist its negative impact on political instability, lack of social cohesion among ethnic groups in

African countries, and incessant civil wars.

Lastly, colonial rule was so pervasive in SSA that no country in the region was completely unaffected. Even Liberia was associated with the American Colonization Society, and Ethiopia briefly came under Italian rule in the last century. Hence, an analysis of the way and manner in which African leadership institutions and governance systems have evolved cannot be complete without examining colonial leadership strategies and their merits and demerits. This shall be our focus in the next chapter

5

COLONIAL LEADERSHIP STRATEGIES: MERITS AND DEMERITS

Chapter 5

Western virtues are not nearly so obvious and easily imitated as vices

– World Christian Handbook 1949, 150f

In the preceding chapter, we examined the economic, cultural, and political reasons for colonization. We now understand that the British intended to "civilize" the peoples of Africa, but not to the extent where the people might demand equal rights with the British. Likewise, the French wanted to turn Africans into French people after the colonization process. The assimilated Africans could then become part of the French community. The Portuguese wanted to create a new society that would include acculturated Africans, with preferably Portuguese ancestry. The Belgians had no specific vision of what they intended for the Africans or what type of future relationship they wanted to have with them. Moreover, the promises of acculturation made to African évolués were never fulfilled. Therefore, it appeared that the end product of these colonial experiences would be for the peoples of Africa under the French and

Portuguese rule to be integrated into the European communities. In the British sphere of influence, the Africans would eventually be left alone at the end of the process to govern themselves using leadership ideas learned from their British masters.

To discuss the merits and the demerits of colonial leadership styles in Africa gives us an insight into how each European colonial power tried to tailor-make their administrative strategies to suit their overall objectives in the colonies. In any event, one can identify four distinct administrative styles or leadership strategies adopted by the European powers in their African colonies: Direct rule associated with France, Germany, and Portugal. The indirect rule is associated with Britain. Company rule linked to the Belgians in Congo, and indirect company rule of Cecil Rhodes in southern Africa. Hence, this chapter is devoted to discussing the good and the not-so-good sides of the administrative structures introduced by the colonialists. This will not be an all-dark narrative intended to put down these masters but an objective analysis of the challenges associated with their rule. Again, this chapter takes an axial approach to decompress research by discussing West Africa separately and then East and southern Africa later.

Colonial Leadership Styles in West Africa

Direct Rule

The French and the Germans in West Africa adopted a centralized administrative style called "direct rule." This implied that colonial rule was imposed on the people regardless of their existing political systems or structures. The French governed their colonial empire, including French West Africa, Guinea, and Togoland, from Paris through the governor. The French used African chiefs, but those chiefs were appointed directly by French officials in recognition of their loyalty to France. The chiefs did not come from royal families and were seldom posted to their native regions. Thus, the French never attempted to preserve the existing African political institutions. Interestingly, direct rule was not applied uniformly across French colonies. In the regions ruled by powerful kings, such as Upper Volta, where the Mossi people had powerful chiefs, the French had to make concessions to those chiefs.

At the turn of the last century, the French went ahead to structure their colonial possessions in West Africa. It became French West Africa, administered by a governor-general based in Dakar, Senegal. It consisted of eight colonial territories, namely: Dahomey (Republic of Benin), Mauritania, Senegal, French Soudan (Mali), Ivory Coast, Upper Volta (Burkina Faso), Niger, and Guinea. Each territory had a territorial assembly under the leadership of the governor. Each territory was divided into circles or colonial circles, each under an administrator called Commandant de Cercle.

In some cases, circles were further broken down into subdivisions, each governed by a Chef de Subdivision. After WWI, Togoland (formerly a German colony) had a separate identity of being governed by a French High Commission as a trust territory under the League of Nations. This colonial administration had French civil servants appointed by the government in Paris. All colonial laws emanated from France, and measures enacted by each territorial assembly had to be duly vetted and approved by the French national legislature in Paris.

Indirect Rule

The British would boast that they ventured into sub-Saharan Africa to share their skills and values, hoping that the natives would eventually run their communities based on the knowledge gained from British officials. The British administrative style in West Africa was formulated by a colonial governor called Lord Frederick Lugard. He duly implemented the policies when he was appointed Nigeria's governor-general at the turn of the last century. Lugard dubbed the system "indirect rule." Simply put, the style involved identifying existing power structures, and rulers so identified would be invited, bribed, or coerced to enlist with the colonial administration system. At the same time, they were allowed to retain considerable political influence over their people. In stateless cultures where there were no headmen, the British simply created them for the people. This was how the "warrant chiefs" of Igboland in Nigeria came into existence. The chiefs were expected to enforce local laws, collect taxes, provide cheap labour for colonial projects if required, and be accountable to the British District Officer (DO). British colonies in West Africa included Nigeria, Gold Coast, Sierra Leone, and The Gambia. Each colony was governed by a governor-general appointed by the British government, and he reported directly to the British Colonial Office in London.

Whereas British officials had always maintained that indirect rule was meant to preserve African traditions and political systems, the truth was that the colonialists quickly realized that the colonies were too large to be governed directly without the assistance of local chiefs. As of 1920, Britain controlled a colonial area in Africa forty times its size. One could only imagine the efforts it would take for the outnumbered British officials to administer those colonies directly. This made

African chiefs become important links between the colonial authorities and the people. Since he understood his people's culture, he could be counted on to transmit directives and orders.

Moreover, in places like Nigeria, where there existed powerful local rulers such as the Oba of Benin and the Sultan of Sokoto, some accommodations had to be made to avoid protracted conflicts. Also, by working with these local leaders, the cost of running the colonies was kept low and more revenues were raised locally. With this in mind, people have argued that indirect rule was just a necessity that the British officials managed to transform into a virtue.

Colonial Leadership Styles in East and Southern Africa

Direct Rule

As stated earlier, direct rule was a highly centralized administrative style adopted by the Germans and the Portuguese in their East and Southern African colonies. Portugal's centralized administration in Angola, Nyasaland (Tanzania), and Moçambique (Mozambique) was much harsher to the Africans than that of France in West Africa. When African people started agitating for self-rule, the Portuguese simply declared their colonial possessions of Cape Verde and Guinea Bissau (in West Africa), Angola, Mozambique, as well as São Tome and Principe (southern Africa) as "Overseas Portugal," described as provinces of Portugal separated geographically from Portugal. The inherent meaning of this declaration was that Portugal had no intention of granting self-determination to her colonies. Like the French, however, they too granted a few African citizenships of Portugal, but the exercise was later curtailed. Eventually, the Portuguese dictator Antonio de Oliveira Salazar (1932 - 1968) declared that Portugal and her colonial possessions constituted "only one state, one territory, one population, one citizenship, and one government." This policy objective alienated African leaders and led them to reject Portuguese imperialism.

The German colonial rule was the briefest among the colonial regimes in Africa, having started in the late 1880s and foreclosed with the signing of the Treaty of Versailles (in 1919), following their defeat in the First World War Nevertheless, the German presence cannot be overlooked given the indelible impact it had on the territories it controlled. Germany's colonial administrative structure was also highly centralized. The German governors were assisted by African subordinates handpicked without regard to existing political power structures in the respective areas they held sway. In areas where the Africans had no chiefs, the Germans simply created one to assist them in the administration of the place. As latecomers into the colonial game, the Germans frantically went into their colonies with the sole intention of economically exploiting the areas as quickly as possible. To this end, their private entrepreneurs and military officers were empowered to exploit the colonies and deal ruthlessly with any opposition from Africans. The African resistance to this brazen attempt at subjugation was seen in the Maji Maji Rebellion (1905 - 1908) in Tanganyika, in which about 120,000 Africans were said to have lost their lives.

Indirect Rule

The British made indirect rule the centrepiece of their colonial administration in Africa. They simply retained existing local power structures to sustain colonial rule. In Tanganyika, where there were no chiefs, they proceeded to create entirely new "tribes" and "chiefs" in line with the objectives of the indirect rule system.

One notable political consequence of the indirect rule policy was that it stunted the development of national political consciousness and enhanced separate ethnic identities. Indeed, the approach served British colonial interests very well, allowing them to play African ethnic groups against one another in a classic divide and rule strategy. Inter-ethnic interactions through political organizations were severely discouraged. The British feared that national associations might lead to nationwide resistance to colonialism. Therefore, it was unrealistic for anyone to have expected ethnic groups with no prior political interactions to forge a united nation when independence came. Widespread incidences of interethnic political violence in former British colonies of Zimbabwe, Zambia, Kenya, Uganda, and South Africa could be partly traced to indirect rule

Table 4: Decolonization in sub-Saharan Africa

Imperial power	Country (former name)	Independence
France	Benin (Dahomey)	1960
	Burkina Faso (Upper Volta)	1960
	CAR (Ubangi Chari)	1960
	Chad	1960
	The Comoros	1975 (except Mayotte Island)
	Congo (French Congo)	1960
	Cote d'Ivoire (Ivory Coast)	1960
	Djibouti (French Somaliland)	1977
	Gabon	1960
	Guinea	1958
	Madagascar	1960
	Mali (Soudan)	1960
	Niger	1960
	Senegal	1960
Britain	Botswana (Bechuanaland)	1966
	The Gambia	1965
	Ghana (Gold Coast)	1957
	Kenya	1963
	Lesotho (Basutoland)	1966
	Malawi (Nyasaland)	1964
	Mauritius	1968
	Nigeria	1960
	Seychelles	1976
	Sierra Leone	1961
	Swaziland	1968
	Uganda	1962
	Zambia (Northern Rhodesia)	1964
	Zimbabwe (Southern Rhodesia)	1980 (UDI 1965)

Britain and Italy	Somalia	1960
Union of British Colonies and the Boer Republic	South Africa	1910 (majority rule in 1994)
Germany, then Belgium from 1916	Burundi (Urundi)	1962
Germany, then Britain/France from 1918	Cameroon	1960
Germany, then South Africa mandate from 1920	Namibia (South West Africa)	1990
Germany, then Belgium from 1916	Rwanda (Ruanda)	1962
Germany, then Britain from 1919; Germany, then Britain, and France from 1919	Tanzania – union of Tanganyika and Zanzibar: (Tanganyika) (Zanzibar)	(1961) (1964)
Belgium	Congo DR (Belgian Congo)	1960
Spain	Equatorial Guinea (Fernando Po and Rio Muni)	1968

Italy	Eritrea	Federated to Ethiopia 1952, Independent 1993
Portugal	Angola Cape Verde Guinea Bissau Mozambique Sao Tome and Principe	1975 1975 1974 1975 1975
None	Ethiopia	—
None	Liberia	—

Company Rule

Company Rule by Belgium in the Congo is associated with the most brutal form of colonial rule in SSA. Initially, the Congo Free State was established as a private fiefdom of King Léopold II of Belgium, who was desirous of taking possession of the land for himself. So, the country did not start as an official colonial territory per se.

However, despite the glamorous name (Congo Free State), the place was neither free nor a state in the real sense. The King simply gave free rein to Belgian businessmen and traders seeking quick profits to exploit the land. They had a license to subjugate the land and the people without being accountable to anyone except King Léopold. His major interest was probably the hefty royal payments made into his coffers.

This type of colonial rule in the Congo featured extensive exploitation of the land, forced labour, and virtual slavery. Africans who resisted being conscripted for work in the labour camps or who did not work hard enough were either flogged in public or had their limbs cut off.

The treatment of Africans was so harsh that even other colonial powers were forced to criticize the Belgian King and urged him to do something about the situation. Lord Hailey brought the scale of atrocities into the public domain when he said, "If Belgium was to avoid further international pressure and the possibility of intervention by more powerful neighbouring powers, then it was necessary for her to establish an administrative and judicial regime in the Congo which could obviate occurrences such as those which had brought the Free State under such hostile criticism."

Also, African-Americans led by W. E. B. DuBois responded to reports of this brutality by raising the issue at the 1st Pan-African Conference held in London in July 1900 and followed it up with petitions to Belgium complaining about the ill-treatment meted to the Congolese on their land.

Due to widespread condemnations of Company Rule in the Congo, a commission of enquiry was appointed to look into the complaints. As a result of its findings, the territory was annexed by Belgium as a formal colony in 1908, putting an end to Company Rule.

By 1919, the other colonial powers, such as Britain and France, appeared to have been impressed enough by what Belgium was doing in the Congo, and they added Burundi and Rwanda (former German colonies) to the Belgian empire as trust territories under the League of Nations. In this arrangement, an administrative system involving Belgian businessmen, traders, and missionaries from the Roman

Catholic Church was put in place. While the businessmen were still in charge of administration, the clergy took charge of missionary education. The Congolese could read and write, but they were never trained beyond the missionary class to engage in scientific research and take charge of their country after the colonialists had left.

Company Rule in the Congo saw the massive transfer of African wealth to Belgium. In return, the Congolese receive limited education. When independence came in 1960, DR Congo exemplified an irony: it had a high literacy rate due to missionary education, but only one college graduate. In essence, the Congo represents colonial ineptitude - it was the least prepared for self-rule in Africa. It has continued to be among the worst governed countries in the world, despite having abundant reserves of natural resources.

Indirect Company Rule

The indirect company rule was associated with Cecil John Rhodes, a British entrepreneur who arrived in southern Africa from Britain in the late 1800s. Rhodes (after whom the scholarships to Oxford University were named) had the ultimate ambition to see British colonial rule extended from Cape Town to Alexandria. From 1885 to 1895, besides making vast fortunes from trades in diamond and gold, he had also acquired two countries Northern Rhodesia (Zambia) and Southern Rhodesia (Zimbabwe), that bore his name. He proceeded to give British protection to Botswana and Malawi, kept Lesotho independent, prevented Paul Kruger's Transvaal from expanding beyond its borders, and almost wrest control of Mozambique from the Portuguese. Rhodes obtained a mining agreement through treachery, the Rudd Concession, which effectively put Zimbabwe under British rule. Armed with the concession, Cecil Rhodes set up his private company, the British South Africa Company, and got a royal charter.

The charter empowered him to govern Malawi, Zambia, and Zimbabwe, where they hoisted the Union Jack in Salisbury (Harare) as the capital base on September 12, 1890. After violent clashes with the local Ndebele and Shona people, the company set up a colonial administration, complete with police, tax collection, and other bureaucracy based on the British indirect rule policy. The company's political functionaries reported to the British Colonial Office in London as if they were normal government appointees. By 1923, the Rhodes colonies of Northern and Southern Rhodesia became self-governing colonies, which allowed the settlers to govern the places independent of the British Colonial Office. This and other developments prompted African nationalist movements in Botswana, Lesotho, Malawi, Zambia, and Zimbabwe to renew African rule agitation.

Distinguishing Features of Direct Rule

1. African chiefs were not leaders of their people but mere political appointees supervised by European officials.

2. African chiefs were not local government authorities in the real sense. They could not perform judicial functions nor enforce laws, except when permitted by the European colonialists.

3. Appointment to the colonial service was not by birth but by education or loyalty to the colonial cause.

4. African chiefs could be transferred from one place to another within a colony. This policy particularly destroyed traditional paramountcy.

Features of Indirect Rule

1. Indirect rule enabled the extension of British colonial rule to a relatively large area in Africa subject to British authority.

2. Smaller ethnic groups were incorporated into larger and more highly organized groups.

3. District heads were appointed for stateless African societies without considerations for the people's feelings.

4. Tyrannical rulers were sustained in many places in so far as they remained loyal to the British Crown, which promoted divisions among the people.

5. The tyranny of the British-appointed warrant chiefs often led to protests in places Like Tivland, Igboland, Ibibio land, and Ghana.

6. Indirect rule weakened Africa's traditional political system and transformed local rulers into mere assistants to British colonial officials. They were treated as government employees rather than as advisers or collaborators.

7. It also substantially excluded the educated African elite from the colonial government and native administration, thus turning them into an alienated class. It rather preserved old conservative rulers who did not have the education to cope with the changing political landscape.

Features of Company and Indirect Company Rule

1. Company rule and indirect company rule were respectively associated with the Belgians in Congo and Cecil Rhodes in

southern Africa. These were colonial systems administered mainly by European businessmen and their employees.

2. Under these systems, brutal and extensive exploitation of African resources was rampant. The wealth made therein was transferred to Europe for the benefit of the companies' stakeholders.

3. Company rule in Congo allowed the church, especially the Roman Catholic Church, to play more active roles in the colonial administration.

4. Political functionaries were in the employ of private companies, which reported to their home government.

5. It did not consider the empowerment of Africans with education for self-rule.

Demerits and Merits of Colonial Rule in Africa

The specific economic and socio-political practices of colonialism lend credence to the political theory of imperialism, which implies that colonization had to do with the subjugation of Africans and little to do with religion. We have shown clearly that there were a few other dimensions to colonialism and that there is a correlation among the factors involved - be it economic or political. Demerits and merits of colonialism will be briefly discussed hereunder such themes as:

- Usurpation of the African traditional political system

- Expropriation of African land

- Unfair taxation

- Exploitation and conscription of labour

- Introduction of cash crops

- Destruction of African culture and value system

- Prohibition of inter-African interactions

- Introduction of Western education and medicine

Demerits

Usurpation of African Traditional Political System

Investigations of the colonial administrative styles like direct rule and indirect rule have revealed how colonialism led to the usurpation of the role of local rulers and chiefs as leaders of their people. The Europeans turned African kings into their subordinates. In places where the chiefs resisted European domination, they were attacked, tricked, killed, or deposed, or sent into exile, while pliant chiefs were appointed to replace them.

Expropriation of African Land

The importance of land to African communal life cannot be overemphasized. In African societies, land was communally owned, and people could only use it but not own it or sell it to foreigners. This tradition of collective ownership of land made African communities particularly sensitive to European appropriation of their land resources. The rationale for taking African land was based on three notions including:

1.   That the land belonged to no one because when the Europeans arrived, no one was using it, even though

generations of Africans might have cultivated the land before moving to another location to give the land enough time to replenish itself.

2.   That Africans have ceded the land to them through treaties, though most of those agreements were signed by local chiefs under duress.

3.   That colonial government had the right to take any land in the public interest, though the government was not representative of the African people.

Unfair Taxation

Two reasons have been identified for the introduction of tax regimes in African colonies: one was to coerce more Africans into the colonial labour market, and another was to raise revenue for the running of colonial governments, as well as pay the cost of prosecuting WWI and WWII. The taxes had to be paid in European currency, and Africans had to either join the colonial labour force or work as clerks in colonial-run establishments to get the money. In this regard, the taxes forced many Africans to sign up for work.

Exploitation and Conscription of Labour

After African lands had been seized by the European colonizers, it soon became apparent that they did not have the numbers to till the land and would have to generate labour from the local populace. With time, some Africans signed up as labourers for white farmers or mines owners.

Working conditions were appalling, and wages were meagre. It often took a male worker and his family to complete a day's allotment of work. Only male workers were paid, partly in cash and partly in food rations at the end of the day.

Labour shortage plagued African colonial governments, especially between the two world wars. Therefore, forced labour conscription was introduced as a colonial policy. African chiefs were enlisted to produce assigned quotas of labourers to work on plantations, harbours, railroads, roads, mines, and other capital projects. For instance, over 40,000 labourers were conscripted to work in Rhodesian mines between the 1920s and the 1950s on an annual basis. More than 30,000 of these African workers perished in the mines between 1900 and 1933 alone.

Three consequences of labour conscription include the resultant disruption of the African way of life caused by the practice by as able-bodied men were separated from their families; the shortage of productive workforce, and the resultant famine in many African villages since the draft took away healthy young men who could cultivate the land for food production; and the alienation of local chiefs (engaged as conscripts) from their people - a development that ultimately undermined traditional leadership institutions. This proved regrettable later in history and made the task of nation-building much more difficult in Africa.

Prohibition of Inter-African Interactions

Before colonization, African people had been trading and interacting with one another for millenniums. However, with the advent of colonization, inter-African interactions came to an abrupt end with the portioning of Africa into different colonial territories. Following the unfortunate scenario, trade and communications were now carried out only with their respective European masters. British colonies traded with Britain, Portuguese colonies with Portugal, French colonies with France, and others. African countries became sources of raw materials for European factories, and this trade was heavily skewed in favour of Europe. It also became impossible for two Africans living in two towns separated by a colonial boundary to communicate directly with each other on the phone. Their phone call would have to be routed through a European capital first and at prohibitive costs. A direct consequence of this was that African communities and countries were cut off from one another. Even today, for instance, it is still easier to fly from Lagos to London than it is from Lagos to Kinshasa. And what's more, African countries could not trade with each other since most of them produced similar mineral resources and agricultural products introduced by their colonial masters.

Other Negative Impacts of Colonialism on Africans Include:

- The destruction of African culture through the imposition of foreign religions and the resultant attacks on the African value system mounted by missionary schools, which contributed in no small way to the loss of confidence in themselves and their heritage.

- Retardation of post-colonial political development as the denial of political participation and discouragement of inter-ethnic interactions among Africans inhibited post-colonial political development. It promoted the use of force to settle political scores after that.

Arbitrary boundaries

The imperialists' imposition of arbitrary state borders on the African continent had dire consequences. The trouble lies with the fact that, when they were delineated, these state boundaries rarely matched existing pre-colonial political, social, or economic divisions. They were arbitrary because they reflected the short-term economic and strategic interests of the imperial powers rather than the interests of indigenous Africans.

A glance at the modern map of Africa, for example, clearly shows an external instead of internal logic to the chosen criteria. Many of the boundaries are ruler-straight, following lines of longitude and latitude. Historically determined political divisions such as the state borders of Europe do not resemble this.

There are other sore points. Why was German South-West Africa (Namibia), for example, awarded a narrow strip of land (the Caprivi Strip) to its North-East, and why does West Africa host the tiny state of The Gambia? In the first instance, Namibia's odd shape was a result of the strategic requirements of Germany's Foreign Minister, Count von Caprivi. He insisted that this territory should have access to the Zambesi River to deploy a gunboat. The second case arose because British commercial interests had established a trading post at the mouth of the River Gambia. Despite French pressure, the British government refused to give up this territory. Consequently, The Gambia is a micro-state, no more than 50 kilometres wide at any point, and entirely enclosed by Senegal (except for its short coastline.)

Then there is the curious case of Cabinda. This oil-rich enclave is part of Angola. Yet, the Democratic Republic of Congo separates it from greater Angola. This is because King Léopold of Belgium insisted that his African kingdom should adjoin the Atlantic Ocean.

Additionally, it is important to stress that if African state borders had reflected 'natural' economic or political divisions rather than these arbitrary and snap-of-finger impositions, these abnormalities would not have become indelible stains on the contemporary map of Africa.

As the British Prime Minister of the day, Lord Salisbury, quipped at an 1890 Anglo-French conference: 'we have been engaged in drawing lines upon maps where no white man's foot ever trod; we have been giving away mountains and rivers and lakes to each other, only hindered by the small impediment that we never knew exactly where the mountains and rivers and lakes were.' Salisbury's after-dinner joke loses its humour when contextualized in the light of the problems that these 'arbitrary' borders created for post-colonial Africa.

The majority of these boundaries do not make any economic sense, and in addition to the initial disruption to intra-ethnic and inter-ethnic communication and trade lines, the colonially foisted boundaries did result in long-term problems for the African States.

Decisions made in European capital cities in the late 18th Century, for instance, have led to 16 SSA countries being landlocked, including Botswana, Burundi, Burkina Faso, Central African Republic, Chad, Ethiopia, Lesotho, Malawi, Mali, Niger, Rwanda, South Sudan, Swaziland, Uganda, Zambia, and Zimbabwe. No other continent is home to so many landlocked countries as the African continent.

In terms of trade, this places a state at a great disadvantage because they have to perpetually rely on their neighbours' willingness and altruism to convey the bulk of their exports and imports.

Alongside economic obstacles, Africa's artificial boundaries have also precipitated political and social problems as colonial borders ran through existing political and social units. In this sense, colonial rule 'dehumanized' Africa's borders.

This failure of the imposed boundaries to recognize existing divisions was at the root of two major problems for Africa's post-colonial governments.

First, there was the possibility of irredentism. Irredentism is the desire to unite under one flag a community that is currently divided. If a pre-colonial political unit found itself split between two states, then there was always a danger that, after independence, violence would be used to reunite this community.

For instance, Somalia unsuccessfully went to war with Ethiopia in the 1970s to win the Ogaden - an area populated by ethnic Somalis. The government in Mogadishu wanted to house all the Somali people within the boundaries of just one sovereign state.

The second potential problem is the possibility of internal ethnic conflicts within a state. Imperial boundaries not only split social groups but also caged them together within these artificially new nation-states. For example, over 250 ethnic groups reside within the boundaries of Nigeria alone. Post-colonial states were thus forced to create institutions and political procedures that ensured that any conflict among their socially divided populations could be resolved peacefully.

Reinforcing the Non-Hegemonic State

As well as producing arbitrary boundaries, European colonialism also reinforced the non-hegemonic nature of the African state. In Sub-Saharan Africa, for example, only in Kenya, South Africa, Southern Rhodesia, and South-West Africa were their pretensions at building a modern state, with each of these territories receiving significant numbers of white settlers. In the rest of the region, the imperial powers had only limited goals. There was no desire to invest resources to ensure the state could project its authority into every corner of the new colonies. Instead, they only concentrated on economically productive or strategically important regions.

A minimal infrastructure was built, backed by a few European administrators and troops, but the imperial governments were not prepared to implement the theories of the 'civilizing mission' proclaimed by the explorers and missionaries of the 18th Century. This was colonization on the cheap. No wholesale economic or political development was planned for the colonial territories.

Despite the massive impact this period of European colonialism would have on African political systems, the actual penetrative capacity of African states was relatively weak. As would be observed later, this lack of state capacity was a legacy that post-colonial governments had difficulty overcoming.

Weak Links Between Government and The Governed

A natural consequence of this lack of state penetration was that at independence, African countries inherited weak links between the government and the people. The colonial political authority had been gained on the continent through conquest and political institutions imposed. Coercion was a substitute for legitimacy. The state and, by extension, government, in this regard, never rested on a social contract between the government and the people.

Indeed, colonial administrators were not even accountable to the Africans they ruled. Instead, they obeyed orders emanating from their superiors back in the capitals of Europe. Therefore, the government was solely about maintaining order, balancing budgets, and overseeing the extraction of raw materials for export. It was never about the provision of public services for citizens. For this reason, Crawford Young described the African colonial states as 'alien to their core.'

In contrast, stronger links between the government and the people developed more naturally within the modern Western state. There, institutions had grown out of and shaped by their society.

Over centuries, elements of civil society had competed with emperors and monarchs, resulting in first the middle class and then the working-class gaining empowerment. Each group eventually succeeded in shaping state institutions to reflect their demands. Today, notions of democracy underpin this relationship between the state and society, and a complex provision of public services has resulted.

This contrasts strongly with the situation in sub-Saharan Africa, where the modern state arrived almost overnight, and its nature owed little to existing indigenous civil society. Africans were simply left out of any representative relationship between the government and the people.

This situation did not bode well for a successful interaction between the state and society in post-colonial Africa.

Merits

As to whether colonization ultimately benefited Africans is a subject of much controversy among social scientists; it is an issue that may never be resolved. For our discussion on colonial leadership styles, I shall highlight some of what I perceive as the positive contributions of colonialism to African life. By so doing, however, I have no intention to whitewash its overwhelming negative impacts.

Introduction of Cash Crops

The whites introduced cash crops such as cashew, cocoa, cotton, coffee, oil palm, sisal, and tea into many African countries. West African countries like Cameroon, Ghana, Ivory Coast, and Nigeria, which were suitable for growing cocoa and oil palm, specialized in these crops, and they have continued to reap the benefits to date. Kenya and Uganda cultivated coffee, cotton, and tea; Tanzania produced cotton and sisal. These crops have served as major sources of foreign exchange earnings in these places for close to a century.

Introduction of Formal Education

The introduction of formal education by mission schools deserves mention as it helped to unlock the hidden potential of Africans and broaden the people's worldview. Nearly all African leaders (from Nkrumah to Mandela) who emerged after WWII to lead their countries toward independence got their organizational and rhetorical skills from Western education. Some of the moral and political principles with which they challenged and fought colonialism were rooted in Western education and philosophy.

Infrastructural Interventions

No matter how small, the few infrastructures provided by colonial authorities became the foundation upon which African leaders built their newly independent nations. Electric power, harbours, roads, railroads, telephones, radio services, and water supply systems were constructed to service the colonial government. By working for the colonial bureaucracies, Africans acquired important skills, which became handy at and after independence.

Shortening the Process of State Formation

The colonial rule imposed arbitrary boundaries on Africans, and countries were created to suit the fancy of colonial officials. However, when everything is considered, this might have helped shorten the process of state formation across Africa, which would have been otherwise slow and painful since powerful African leaders were already waging brutal wars against their weaker neighbours. After all, the history of inter-ethnic conflicts in Africa is well documented.

Conclusion

If there is something we can deduct from this chapter is that European powers abrogated African leadership institutions and introduced new governance systems amenable to their interests. For example, Britain adopted the Indirect Rule system by which Africans were ruled through their leaders or colonial surrogates under the control of the British colonial government. In contrast, the French, another major colonial power, adopted the Direct Rule policy of assimilation, which aimed to integrate French colonial territories into the main French government in Paris. In Belgium-Congo and other places, we saw a most dehumanizing form of colonial administration in the form of Company Rule. Africans and their resources were atrociously exploited by companies owned by wealthy European merchants, who either pay local chiefs peanuts to take over their land or confiscate such property. Unfair taxation, conscription and exploitation of local labour, expropriation of African land, and prohibition of inter-African trade are some of the negative impacts of these colonial administrative strategies.

In terms of governance, colonization engendered military incursion into politics and other forms of illegitimate rule. The colonial governors were brutally autocratic rather than representative. In all cases, existing traditional African governance systems, as well as their inbuilt checks and balances, were destroyed by the colonial governments. Traditional rulers who were development planners of their societies were stripped of their powers and made to work as civil servants in the colonialists' interest. Those chiefs who resisted colonial rule were simply removed by the colonial officials and replaced with submissive ones. Hence, neither the European colonial officials nor the new African colonial chiefs were accountable to the people. This socio-political dislocation of the traditional governance system and its adverse impacts on Africans and African society will be discussed in subsequent chapters.

However, Colonial Rule in Africa was not all gloom and doom as it also brought some notable positive developments in terms of the formation of nation-states from hitherto disparate ethnic groups, the introduction of judicial and bureaucratic institutions, the introduction of formal education, the introduction of cash crops and plantation agriculture with other modern farming techniques.

Nevertheless, the demerits of colonization far outstripped its merits since it was a painful experience for Africans – an experience that cost them a lot in terms of environmental degradation, loss of lives, mineral and material exploitation, and psychological put-down of being labelled "an inferior race." Moreover, the leadership strategies imposed on SSA by those Western imperialists failed to transmute it from underdevelopment to development. After all, it is difficult to find any evidence and plausible counterfactuals to argue that countries in today's Africa have developed because Europeans colonized it. Quite the contrary!

6

ANALYZING WESTERN LEADERSHIP ORIENTATION AND ITS IMPACT ON AFRICA

Chapter 6

So far, we have seen how colonialism nay Western imperialism negatively impacted leadership institutions and broadly disrupted governance systems in sub-Saharan Africa. This chapter will be devoted to the analysis of Western leadership orientation and its impacts on Africa. I will also try to highlight why these foreign perspectives are inimical to Africa's progress and development.

An Overview of Western Leadership Concepts

Leadership has been the subject of debate and essays for many centuries, but it is only in the last century that it became a topic for sustained academic research. Many theories of leadership have also been developed during the previous 70 years or so. Like most other theories of human behaviour, however, ways of testing these theories and establishing their scientific accuracy have remained largely elusive. The result is that such theories can only be assessed in respect of the intuitive appeal of the explanations they offer rather than by their ability to withstand repeated attempts to falsify predictions made from them following conventional forms of scientific investigation.

Prevailing Western functional views of leadership are closely associated with organizational culture questions, and it is sometimes stated that the culture of an organization can be remoulded by top management. Leaders - transformative leaders in particular - are seen as harbingers of positive cultural values and catalysts of constructive change. It is fashionable for Western leaders to lead from the front, so their leaders are visible role models who use their actions to show what they expect from others. A particularly crucial aspect of the leader's role is to set the tone for the organization by promoting desirable attributes and values, which are the building blocks of organizational culture. Clues to desirable organizational values could be found in corporate mission and vision statements. Reference is often made to the importance of values such as acceptance of and willingness to admit mistakes, fairness, commitment to the organization, productivity, quality, good customer relations, trust, and honesty.

In the prevailing Western functionalist paradigm, transformational leaders pay close attention to trust, which ensures the reliability of employee actions and further reduces the need for supervision. They also set the organization's direction and shape employee behaviour by outlining a vision that is persuasive enough to inspire others in its pursuit. This principle assumes that employees will take initiatives of their own volition once the organization's goals have been set.

Because the possession of a vision by an organization is seen to be essential to effective transformational leadership in the Western sense, its requisite ingredients have been said to be:

• Different in such a way as to reconstitute the known;

• Aware that its realization is dependent on the contribution of others; and

- Be a vision the leader breathes and lives.

This last criterion raises pertinent questions of authenticity and integrity, which are central to the idea of the transformational leader. In his typically forthright way, the foremost scholar on management theories, Prof. Mant, noted that the 'management' demands of most management jobs are not particularly onerous, but leadership (which involves sticking your neck out and some moral fortitude) seems to be a more elusive quality. Another scholar, Mintzberg, regarded authenticity as the most crucial ingredient of culture-building and leadership.

In the West, leaders have a visible role, leading from the front, which expresses their intention in doing things and their expectation of followers' works. One of the most important aspects of Western leadership roles is conveying and promoting desirable values such as equality, honesty, trust, quality, and efficiency.

Western leadership stimulates the organization's desirable values and trust as the requirement of supervision and control. A Western leader is expected to display ethical behaviour, including sincerity of purpose and integrity, which are important features that bestow legitimacy on leadership.

It is the job of a Western leader to set the psychological tone of the organization by articulating those desirable and requisite values for building an organizational culture. Again, setting directions for organizations is a common choice of Western leaders as a way of inspiring their staff to set and achieve goals effectively.

Current Western leadership theories and rhetoric also place a high premium on empowerment, teamwork, delegation, learning, listening, performance, management, and rationality. The problem is that the hype surrounding such putative management features implies that it is a hard sell, even in its place of origin. Transformational leadership in the West is more a construct of management consultants' rhetoric than it is the reality of management practice. The less the value of the product to the consumer, the more its hype, which helps to disguise its ineffectiveness in most of the cultures where its tenets are applied.

Hofstede's Cultural Dimensions Theory

Hofstede's Cultural Dimensions Theory, propounded in 1980 by Geert Hofstede, a Dutch management researcher, is a framework developed to study the differences in culture across countries and understand how business can be managed across diverse cultural settings. In other words, the framework can be used to distinguish between different national cultures, the dimensions of culture and assess their impacts on a business environment. According to Hofstede, the six dimensions of culture are:

(1)   **Power Distance Index (PDI):** A higher degree of the Index indicates that hierarchy is established and executed in society, without doubt, or reason. A lower degree of the Index signifies that the people question authority and attempt to distribute power.

(2)   **Individualism Index (IDV):** This index explores the "degree to which people in a society are integrated into groups." Individualistic societies have loose ties that often only relate an individual to their immediate family. They emphasize the "I" versus the "We." Its counterpart, collectivism, describes a society in which closely integrated relationships tie extended families and others into in-groups. These in-groups are laced with undoubted loyalty and support each other when a conflict arises with another in-group.

(3) **Uncertainty Avoidance Index (UAI):** Societies that score a high degree in UAI opt for stiff codes of behaviour, guidelines, laws and generally rely on absolute truth or the belief that one line of truth dictates everything people ought to know.

A lower degree in this index shows more acceptance of differing thoughts or ideas. Society tends to impose fewer regulations, ambiguity is more accustomed to, and the environment is more free-flowing.

(4) **Masculinity Index (MAS):** In this dimension, masculinity refers to "a preference in society for achievement, heroism, assertiveness, and material rewards for success." Its counterpart represents "a preference for cooperation, modesty, caring for the weak, and good quality of life." Women in their respective societies tend to display different values. In feminine societies, they share modesty and caring views equally with men. In more masculine societies, women are somewhat assertive and competitive, but notably less than men. In other words, they still recognize a gap between male and female values. This dimension is frequently viewed as taboo in highly masculine societies.

(5) **Long Term Orientation Index:** This dimension associates the past with the present and future actions/challenges. A lower degree of this index (short term) indicates that traditions are honoured and kept while steadfastness is valued. Societies with a high degree in this index (long-term) view adaptation and circumstantial, pragmatic problem-solving as a necessity. A poor country that is short-term oriented usually has little or no economic development, while long-term oriented countries continue to develop to a level of prosperity.

(6) **Indulgence Index (IND):** This dimension refers to the degree of freedom that societal norms give citizens to fulfil their

human desires. Indulgence can be defined as "a society that allows relatively free gratification of basic and natural human desires related to life enjoyment and fun." Its counterpart is designed as "a society that controls gratification of needs and regulates it using strict social norms."

Figure 3: Illustration of Hofstede's Six Cultural Dimensions

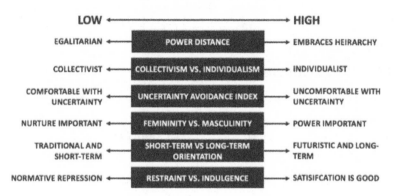

Source from www.corporatefinanceinstitute.com

Root of Differences

According to Hofstede, leaders, followers, consultants, and management are all human. Therefore, their research reflects the limitations of their societies - the particular cultures in which they grew up. Since leadership and management have a reciprocal relationship, as well as share common essential factors, the existence of a linkage between culture and leadership is undeniable. Consequently, it is reasonable to believe that the differences mentioned above between Afrocentric and Western leadership are traceable to the differences in the two disparate cultures.

Comparison of the six dimensions of culture between selected African and Western countries

Table 5.1 Power Distance Index:

Western Nations			African Countries	
Nations	PDI		Countries	PDI
USA	**40**		Nigeria	80
UK	35		Angola	83
Germany	**35**		Tanzania	70

Table 5.2 Individualism Index:

Western Nations			African Countries	
Nations	II		Countries	II
USA	**91**		Nigeria	30
UK	89		Angola	18
Germany	**67**		Tanzania	25

Table 5.3 Masculinity Index:

Western Nations			African Countries	
Nations	MI		Countries	MI
USA	**62**		Nigeria	60
UK	66		Angola	20
Germany	**66**		Tanzania	40

Table 5.4 Uncertainty Avoidance Index:

Western Nations		African Countries	
Nations	UAI	Countries	UAI
USA	**46**	Nigeria	55
UK	35	Angola	60
Germany	**65**	Tanzania	50

Table 5.5 Long Term Orientation Index:

Western Nations		African Countries	
Nations	LTOI	Countries	LTOI
USA	**26**	Nigeria	13
UK	51	Angola	15
Germany	**83**	Tanzania	34

Table 5.6 Indulgence Index:

Western Nations		African Countries	
Nations	InI	Countries	InI
USA	**68**	Nigeria	84
UK	69	Angola	83
Germany	**40**	Tanzania	38

Aggregated from http://geert-hofstede.com

To illustrate the differences between African-centred and Western leadership, Hofstede's six dimensions of culture are applied. Compared to their Western counterparts under Hofstede's cultural dimensions, selective African countries are illustrated in Table 5.7.

To start with, the PDI shows very high scores for SSA countries. On the other hand, selected Western countries do have a lower power distance (40 for the USA and 35 for both Germany and the UK). On the IDV index, African countries have relatively low ratings showing a high level of collectivism; figures for SSA depict a high level of individuality. Moving to the UAI, the table shows medium masculinity in almost all the countries except the UK, which is much lower.

The LTO index shows that while SSA countries are mostly short-term in orientation, the Westerners are much more long-term oriented than their African counterparts, except the USA, with a rating of 26. On the IND index, the African countries of Nigeria and Angola have very high ratings except for Tanzania. In contrast, Europeans have medium ratings except for Germany, whose rating is below average.

In the light of Hofstede's framework, it is unlikely that more than a handful of the more than 40 countries in sub-Saharan Africa, many of whose cultures have not been adequately studied using Hofstede's dimensions, would have cultural profiles conducive to the existing leadership theory now prevalent in the West. Besides, we can deduct from the foregoing that while Western leadership theory may not always be suitable for Africa, the persuasiveness of the message is often difficult to resist, particularly in the absence of local alternatives. The next chapter shall be devoted to outlining leadership styles that are more in tune with African cultural realities and past experiences to counterbalance. For now, however, let us illustrate the fundamental differences between African and Western cultures.

To summarize the discussion, here are some of the major differences in how people prefer to act when it comes to working and thinking in Western and African societies.

Western Leadership Principles: Assumptions and Implications

As with Western functionalist notions of organization and development, which place great emphasis on things like teamwork and interpersonal skills, rather than the organizational design itself, which gives much consideration to differentials of reward and structure, current Western rhetoric on leadership also suggests that its underlying values attach considerable importance to the following attributes:

- High tolerance of ambiguity on the part of all concerned;

- High levels of trust;

- The relative equality of power between leaders and followers;

- A desire to share feelings;

- A willingness to take risks and confront differences of opinion; and

- Strong belief in teamwork.

These values can be translated into Hofstede's dimensions of national culture as:

- Low power distance - the less powerful individuals in a society are unwilling to regard the unequal distribution of power as normal.

- Low individuality - people place a high value on group identity rather than individual identity.

- Low uncertainty avoidance - people are not worried by situations they consider to be unstructured and tend not to believe in absolute truths.

- Medium masculinity - different roles are defined for either sex, meaning that while men are expected to be relatively assertive, women are to serve and care for children.

Common sense and research findings tell us that many countries have cultural profiles that are different from those described above. The apparent fact shows the prescriptive nature of Western leadership theory that these cultural prescriptions do not conform to the cultural profile of the USA, which is characterized by medium power distance, high masculinity, low uncertainty avoidance, and high individualism. When the Western leadership cultural profile was compared to those of African countries among the 53 countries and regions studied by Hofstede in his monumental research, not a single country matched the profile on all four dimensions. Only Costa Rica in North America matched the profile on power distance and individuality, while Jamaica corresponded to uncertainty avoidance and was close to it on masculinity.

To summarize the discussion, here are some of the major differences in how people prefer to act when it comes to working and thinking in Western and African societies.

Table 6: Typical work styles in different societies

Society	Western	SSA
Workstyle	Competitive, quick	Methodical thoughtful
Thinking	"let me try this here first on my own!"	"Let me evaluate this first and then decide to act!"

Table 7: Comparison of Western and African leadership concepts

Element	Western leadership ideal	Indigenous leadership in SSA
Influence on leadership practices	Paramount concern for organizational performance Drive for efficiency and competitiveness Follower-oriented thus participative	Highly centralized power structures Low degrees of uncertainty Emphasis on control mechanisms rather than organizational performance Bureaucratic resistance to change Individual concern for basic security Importance of extended family and kin networks

Managing uncertainty	A high degree of tolerance for ambiguity. The continuous change is viewed as natural and desirable. Sense of urgency.	Deep-rooted, shared theologies and philosophies provide relative certainty and security. Hierarchy and conformity are stressed. Collectivist mutual duties. A long-term view of evolving change.
Managing authority	The relative equality of authority and status between manager and subordinates. Decentralization/ delegation. Teamwork. Empowerment.	Authoritarian/ paternalistic leadership patterns. Centralization. Bureaucratic controls. Preoccupation with rules and procedures. Reluctance to judge performance.
Managing relationships	High levels of trust and openness are valued. The open confrontation of differences. Conflict is valued as potentially creative. Support of followers essential. Drive to secure commitment and high morale.	High degrees of conservatism. Change-resistant organizational hierarchies reinforced my preoccupation with rules. Social networks are crucial to providing individual security.

Source: Blunt & Jones (1997)

Disclaimer: These are generalizations. People have different individual traits that influence their attitudes and behaviours. Thus, this may not be a reflection of everyone but is more of a nuance that we should be aware of when interacting with global counterparts.

Table 7 summarizes some of the elements in the current Western 'ideal' model of leadership discussed here and contrasts them with elements in patterns of leadership in Africa. The intention is to convey some impressions of organizational leadership in SSA and compare them with Western nations' rhetoric of transformational leadership.

It remains to be seen whether these features will be eroded in developing countries in SSA as functions of the more entrenched open-market systems of macro-economic management and emergent middle classes who may favour liberal democratic means of political control.

For the moment, however, it seems that many indigenous managers in developing countries - especially those who trained in the West - will be susceptible to suggestions, in some cases perhaps feeling that things can only get better and assuming, wrongly, that organizational dysfunction in their own countries invalidates all indigenous management practice or local variations of Western practice. However, there is a growing body of empirical evidence that exposes this mistaken assumption and fosters increasing recognition of indigenous forms of governance and organizational systems.

On the other hand, informed expatriate managers may find it less difficult to judge the relevance in foreign leadership models that they find difficult to apply at home. But it will be less straightforward for them to determine what should be put in their place. The functionalist agenda clearly will not be well-served by attempts to engender in Africa forms of leadership which, it could be said, have failed to take hold in the West.

This book suggests that foreign managers working in Africa and indigenous managers interacting with their foreign counterparts should engage with their foreign counterparts, in the expectation that there will be a two-way transfer of know-how, alongside careful joint considerations of which practice makes the most sense in any given set of circumstances.

There is an added risk in all these of romanticizing indigenous leadership concepts - in much the same way as some social anthropologists used to champion the cause of the 'noble savage' - a luxury less easily indulged by the subjects of their concern.

This book also maintains that there is no one best way to manage or lead human resources. I have attempted to show that the "how" and "what" of leadership vary from one region, country, and even culture to another. Therefore, this could be the main reason why Western leadership principles seem to have failed in lifting Africa from its leadership and governance crisis.

The logic of this argument will apply to nations also in so far as their overall character supersedes internal culture variation. Concerning questions of leadership and governance, some countries will prioritize aims over means at certain stages of their development. Others define aims and means somewhat differently, but no better or worse than what the West's concepts connote. As a result, this should lead one to expect, rather than resist on principle, the expression of cultural and institutional differences, which give rise to human resource management and leadership that do not conform smoothly to models now widespread in the Western world.

Issues discussed in this book are expected to be defined, partly in universal and partly in localized terms. Finding a proper balance may be difficult, but evidence supporting the need to do so is compelling.

Colonial Legacy of Leadership Failure in Africa

As political scientists would argue, the leadership failure and poor quality of governance institutions in Africa cannot be discussed outside the historical context of modern African states. From this perspective, the encounters between African societies and European colonialists constitute an essential factor in institution-building in sub-Saharan Africa. It fostered a leadership structure on which future attempts at institutional development would be dependent. Because Western imperialism was driven by the dual logic of exploitation and subjugation, the governance framework that underpinned it was as arbitrary as it was exclusionary and tyrannical. This means that the government structures were designed without considering the interests of the people.

In essence, the European colonial system adulterated and wholly obliterated, in some instances, traditional African institutions of governance while bequeathing artificial colonial states with frail identity or administrative capacity. Without the ability to exercise its authority over different groups in society, some of which seemed more powerful than the government and posed a severe threat to national unity, the post-colonial African leaders resorted to embracing the government philosophy of the colonial era.

In many African countries, the democratic ideology that propelled the struggle for self-rule and independence soon gave way to centralizing logic of authoritarianism in the immediate post-independence era, driven by the imperative to preserve political power. Consequently, the political culture of the new African rulers was strongly influenced by their belief in elitism, nationalism, and statism, which reflected the socializing influences of both the traditional African society and Western imperialism. African business and political leaders of the immediate post-colonial era began to see themselves as possessing a monopoly on legitimacy and wisdom. They had been wired to see the African state and its bureaucracy as all there was to the society, and because of the artificialness of the states that they inherited, these African rulers greatly revered national unity and tended to see any form of political dissent as subversion.

This disposition towards political authority accounts for the prevalence of military regimes or one-party political systems in the immediate post-colonial era in Africa, all of which came at the expense of developing democratic institutions of governance. For instance, it can be argued that the institutional shortcomings that characterized the democratization process in Nigeria in recent times stem partly from long years of military rule, which the country was subjected to. This probably explains why military values continue to permeate Nigeria's political landscape, thus undermining the emergence of dynamic democratic institutions in the country. However, rather than military dictatorship or one-party political system per se, it is the neo-patrimonial character of the modern African state that has survived as the political legacy of Western colonialism and accounts for most African leadership crises across the countries of sub-Saharan Africa.

Neo-patrimonialism combines with legal authority and patrimonial rule to produce a leadership system defined by clientelism, patronage, and a blurring of the line between the private and public sectors.

According to Engelbert and College, "neo-patrimonial policies are ... the equilibrium outcome of illegitimate post-independence statehood, a condition which entails a dichotomization of power and state structures." Neo-patrimonialism emerged as the dominant leadership structure in sub-Saharan Africa because of the superficial nature of the modern African state, which originated outside indigenous social relations and had limited foundations in traditional African society. Therefore, neo-patrimonial policies constitute a political strategy deployed by the ruling elite to secure support for the state by entering into informal alliances with dominant social forces, albeit at the expense of formal state institutions, which are then turned into resources to maintain extensive clientelist networks. Given the personalized nature of politics in neo-patrimonial systems, such systems generally feature low accountability, participation, predictability, and transparency. Thus, although external and internal pressures have forced many African countries to subscribe to the tenets of democracy, and indeed some countries have succeeded in developing relatively functional institutions, yet these political systems constructed to support democratization processes in many countries usually fall victim to the logic of neo-patrimonialism.

Zimbabwe is a glaring case of how an authoritarian logic derived from Western imperialism's legacy has co-existed with a faltering governance experiment for decades, resulting in the emergence of a neo-patrimonial political system. From the historical leadership perspective, the struggle for self-rule in the '60s and '70s can be described as the critical junction in Zimbabwe's history, which established the pattern that would shape the country's development process. The liberation struggle produced a centralized party structure and the future leaders of Zimbabwe. It gave rise to a national ideology of anti-imperialism, which reveres war veterans and remains the country's basic leadership pipeline.

Soon after taking the reins of power in 1980, former President Robert Mugabe and his party, the Zimbabwe African National Union-Patriotic Front (ZANU-PF), embarked on a systematic process of consolidating their grip on power in Zimbabwe. This ambition was achieved by concentrating political power in the office and person of the president while subjecting state institutions to the control of ZANU-PF. To safeguard this political arrangement, an elaborate system of patronage in the form of alliance between the party and the military was established to reward loyalists. In this system, the institutions of governance were subjected to the authority of the party and the president and rendered redundant to further the interests of the former.

A similar neo-patrimonial construct paints an ugly picture of what has been described as the evil triumvirate of non-governance, bad leadership, and excessive governance in many African countries such as Angola, Cameroon, Congo DR, Ivory Coast, Mali, and Nigeria. In Cameroon, government institutions are only public in name but are primarily personal and ineffective in reality. This is the outcome of years of dictatorial rule employed by Cameroon's post-independence rulers to assert authority over a country that was once known for its cultural diversity and economic potential. Since independence, the Cameroonian political system has been characterized by the concentration of political power in the office of the president, enabling both Presidents Ahmadou Ahidjo and Paul Biya to build extensive patronage networks with state resources to secure the loyalty of powerful groups in the polity. Suffice it to say that this institutional framework has been sustained over the years at the expense of a thriving economy, a functional public administration, and democratic culture.

Western Imperialism and Development in Africa

During colonization, the dialectical inter-phase that took place left Africa wrecked culturally, economically, psychologically, and politically. In truth, this period saw Africa under the bondage of economic exploitation, cultural devastation, and socio-political domination. The colonialists destroyed the philosophical base of African cultures and foisted the Western system on them as an alternative.

Amazingly, the legacies of Western imperialism are still prevalent in Africa. For instance, Terrence Rangers' Inventory Theory illustrated the imposition of the Western paradigm on Africa. In the face of the African Renaissance Movement, Rangers put up a new theory of Western imperialism. He argued that whatsoever is rediscovered as African civilizations were European inventions. Hence, there could never be any originality in African identity, and the discoveries were European inventions, especially as the name itself was invented.

The situation of things has allowed Western agents to subtly manipulate the peoples of Africa to see the world from a European lens in all spheres, including economic, scientific, technological, political, and leadership. This deeply engraved mental colonialism has seen many so-called African intellectuals deny Africa's cultural and historical achievements. Some African scholars even rejected the existence of African philosophy during the Great Debate of the 1970s and 1980s.

This Western imperialist propaganda still pervades African political systems, including leadership and governance. This has led to a situation whereby the majority of African leadership development initiatives are hinged on Western ideas and philosophies. Expatriates are routinely invited to manage businesses in Africa, while their African counterparts are encouraged to attend leadership or management programmes in Western schools for them to be seen as qualified enough to assume leadership roles in their organizations. A pertinent question is this: should African leadership development copycat Western leadership development paradigms regardless of the importance of cultural dimensions to leadership?

Many scholars have noted how Western leadership and management theories may represent a new wave of colonialism for Africa – a wave that reinforces thought processes that are rooted in misplaced Western ideologies. By doing so, there is a general tendency to downplay the importance of indigenous knowledge, assuming a linear progression of development from the "traditional" to the modern instead and from the "developing" to the "developed."

However, such an approach to leadership and management theory is pejorative (identifying non-Western approaches as underdeveloped) and inimical to the emergence of more constructive theories or policies.

The ongoing turmoil in Libya, recent race riots in Paris, and the "Black Lives Matter" protests across the United States indicate a growing resistance of populations disenchanted with Western cultural orientations and wholesale imposition in ways that neglect the multicultural world in which we live. But this is just the tip of the iceberg, for every repressed voice potentially carries the answer to the problems we face. In the same way that scientists now travel to remote areas of the world to seek traditional knowledge about the medicinal qualities of plants largely unknown in the West, so do we stand to gain more from the fresh insights offered by examining a different perspective. After all, the Japanese were the ones who used

Edwards Deming's production management ideas to create a strong economy that became the envy of the West, and researchers started looking to the East for new perspectives on leadership and management practices. Given the emphasis placed on social engagement and collective responsibility in traditional African cultures, it is also likely that powerful lessons could be learnt here that could become useful in advancing the concepts of collective and distributed leadership which, while being promoted in Western economy sectors such as education and health, still appear to be elusive in practice.

All we have done so far is to highlight the meaning and impact of the Western leadership paradigm on SSA. We shall now examine the dimensions of Western imperialism in the region.

Dimensions of Western Imperialism in Sub-Saharan Africa

However, at this junction, it is important to mention that imperialism has a political dimension, as well as cultural and material dimensions. Western imperialism succeeded in creating structurally weak nations in SSA and exploited indigenous populations, thus breaking up the material make-up of these societies and culturally destabilizing them. The political aspects of this phenomenon have been asphyxiating. These weak political contraptions created by Western hegemonic tendencies received politico-economic functions at independence, which they were not developed enough to handle.

Judging by Rostow's five stages of development, one will begin to make sense of this assertion. In his historical model of economic growth, the American economist Walt Whitman Rostow postulated that five stages were involved, namely: traditional society, the precondition to take-off, take-off, drive to maturity, and the age of high mass consumption.

Traditional society: This stage of economic development is characterized by subsistence agriculture, primary sector economy, limited application of technology, rigid society, and lack of individual economic mobility.

The precondition to take-off: At this stage, external demand for raw materials initiates economic change. Also, this stage is characterized by the development of more productive agriculture and cash crop cultivation for export, widespread investment in public infrastructures (irrigation, canals, and ports), increasing spread of technology, changing social structure, individual social mobility, and development of national identity, and shared political interests.

Take off: At this stage of development, urbanization increases, technological breakthrough occurs, and industrialization proceeds. The secondary sector expands, and the ratios of primary vs secondary sectors shift towards secondary.

Drive to maturity: Here, there is diversification of the industrial base leading to the establishment of multiple industries—manufacturing shifts from investment-driven or capital goods to consumer durables. Large-scale investments in social infrastructures include universities, schools, technical training institutes, military academies, and hospitals.

Age of Mass Consumption: At this stage, the industrial base dominates the economy, and there exists normative consumption of high-value consumer goods such as automobiles, personal computers, and smartphones. Consumers typically have disposable income for additional goods.

Even though the stated process of development is not sacrosanct as some societies may leap forward or backwards, the point being made in this argument is that every society develops structures that enable it to transit into a new stage of development with new functions. This perspective's beauty is that when societies develop structures, they know the functions these structures are supposed to perform. Hence, societies take on roles based on the structures they have been able to develop.

In this context, Igbo society in the pre-Colonial era serves as a very good example. The Igbos lacked a central authority because of their republican nature and penchant for self-determination. They ran an egalitarian socio-political system in which social security was the order of the day. Achievements and honour were respected above material wealth, and the extended family system was encouraged so that everyone became his brother's keeper. This traditional social order was upended by the advent of Western colonialism into Igboland beginning from the mid-1800s.

Thus, the big question becomes: What if functions are imposed on society from outside? Most African societies were at the "traditional stage" and the "precondition to take-off stage" when the colonialists arrived. The inherent structures in these societies were left as they were to impede resistance and enable the success of the exploitative intentions of the Western imperialists.

Indeed, most African countries at independence were exposed to a world system that they were not matured enough to play the kind of politics inherent in it advantageously. Consequently, they were left at the mercy of Western imperialists who owned and ran the global system in their national interest. This explains why countries like China and Japan once isolated themselves from the world until they were structurally ready to take on the turbulent waters of world politics. The United States is also reckoned to have pursued a policy of isolation or non-intervention at a point in its history.

Coming back to our discussion, the major European powers employed various methods for exploiting African countries, which have, among other dimensions, political, social, and economic dimensions.

Political dimension

Politically speaking, the West established cordial relationships with the African ruling class. This was done to make it easier for these leaders to be used as local agents of imperialism. By installing and supporting puppet leaders in Africa, especially at independence, the colonialists exploited African countries with the active connivance of those petty-bourgeois leaders who often embezzled public funds and banked them overseas, thereby creating more capital for the West. These leaders were satisfied with the crumbs doled out by their imperialist masters while their countries remained impoverished. It is not uncommon for an African political leader to be stupendously wealthy while his constituency wallows in abject poverty.

Moreover, the Western imperialists often tamper with the sovereignty of African countries by organizing coups to overthrow leaders perceived to be anti-imperialist. This informed the tacit support of the West for the coups against Patrice Lumumba of Congo in 1961, Kwame Nkrumah of Ghana in 1966, President Thomas Sankara of Burkina Faso in 1987, and the coup against General Murtala Mohammed in 1976 four weeks after delivering his "Africa has come of age" speech at an extraordinary meeting of the Organization of African Unity (OAU).

Socio-cultural Dimension

The West also utilizes the mass media in the maintenance of an asymmetrical international order. Through major international media organizations like the BBC, CNN, DW, and VOA, the imperialist West disseminated propaganda that psychologically justifies happenings in SSA.

The neo-colonialists also use education to exploit Africa. In the region, the curriculum and language of teaching are informed by imperialistic ideals rather than practical education. Since the colonial era, this has been the case when colonialists were only interested in training Africans to take up clerical positions in colonial governments. Hence, colonialism bequeathed to SSA a system of education that is not based on creativity, productivity, and scientific enquiry but theoretical explanations and paperwork. Therefore, while Western scholars are busy producing and inventing, their African counterparts are busy gathering mere certificates. This reality formed the kernel of Claude Ake's bestseller "Social Science as Imperialism," published in 1982.

Cultural indoctrination is another way in which the West dominates Africa. By using books, magazines, and the mass media, Westerners inculcate their cultural values, including mode of dressing and behaviour, into naive Africans. Through these means, new markets are created for Western products in Africa ostensibly to oil the taste buds of Africans who desire to appear more American or European than African. For example, while Aba in Eastern Nigeria has a thriving, local footwear industry, Nigerians prefer to spend billions of dollars importing American and Italian shoes annually. The same goes for the country's food and textile industries.

Economic dimension

Western nations have so many investments in SSA through multinational corporations (MNCs). Like their 19th Century forerunners, such as the Royal Niger Company and the Guinea Company of Scotland, these companies exploit Africa's markets in collaboration with their local agents. As a classic example, Western corporations were said to control more than 70 per cent of African mineral wealth as of 2008. Not stopping at this, they also controlled the international prices at which these raw materials and mineral resources were sold at the international market. Suffice it to say that they often keep these prices as low as possible to keep African countries in a perpetual unequal exchange situation.

Technology is another economic tool of Western dominance. There is little or no technology transfer from the Western nations to their former colonies in Africa, even in export substitution. For example, many multinationals bring their machinery to work in Africa but do not allow their indigenous or local staff to access the technical know-how of the industrial processes. This means that money made in SSA is spent outside the region because money paid for the machinery and expertise would by design accrue to the West. It is called capital flight.

Western Imperialism in Sub-Saharan Africa: The Cameroonian Experience

Chapter 4 of this book has given a vivid account of how colonialism infiltrated SSA as a form of Western imperialism. The truth is that even after independence, African countries continued to be subjugated by their erstwhile colonial masters, who seemed hell-bent on dominating Africa forever. Here, I will bring into focus the Cameroonian experience, if only to buttress my point.

French influence in Cameroon

As stated earlier, Cameroon was initially a German colony that France and Britain took over after WWI. The annexation was confirmed in the Treaty of Versailles by the League of Nations, which assigned about two-thirds of the territory to France and the rest to Britain. Since its independence from France in 1960, the country has had only two presidents, Ahmadou Ahidjo and Paul Biya, who have ruled for a combined tenure of 60 years.

For France, Cameroon represents a vital source of raw materials for its industries, especially aluminium, bauxite, and oil, and an outlet for capital investments and an important market for manufactured goods. About 70 per cent of the crude oil extracted by French companies comes from Cameroon and other African countries. According to several scholars, France has maintained strong control over Cameroon, which has ensured a favourable environment for French businesses.

Indeed, Cameroon was a centrepiece of French imperialist interests in SSA, together with Gabon, Cote d'Ivoire, and Senegal.

The French influence worked because of a close-knit network of formal and informal colonial institutions, which enabled indirect control over the Cameroonian bureaucracy and the local elite. In this network, the major political decisions regarding SSA lay with the French president and other foreign officials. Economic cooperation and defence pacts ensured that France enjoyed exclusive access to Cameroon's raw materials and prompted asymmetric trade relations. Trading, marketing, and shipping activities are monopolized by French companies resulting in a perpetually favourable trade balance for France. France equally preserved its military influence in

Cameroon in forming a defence partnership agreement and arms supply.

The institutionalization of cultural and linguistic links with Cameroon and other former colonies under the banner of "La Francophone" constituted another reality of French hegemony, reinforcing the assimilation of foreign culture and values by Cameroonians.

Economic Dependence

France retains its overbearing influence on Cameroon in terms of an unfavourable balance of payments and financial control. In 2009 alone, commercial exchanges between the two countries exceeded 1.6 billion USD, but with over 300 million USD trade imbalance for Cameroon. Moreover, many monopolistic practices which were facilitated by colonial bilateral agreements are still ongoing. For instance, the French company, Boloré has primarily monopolized the Cameroonian railway, Camrail, the majority of the Douala Port, and the shipping line to Europe, and the transport per truck service.

Also, there are numerous cases of favourable treatment of French companies, especially concerning the non-suing of legal infractions. Some of the most important issues concern the illegal exploitation of wood. About one-third of Cameroonian logging areas are controlled by French companies, including Bolloré, Coron, Thanry, and Rougier, which, according to Transparency International (TI), acts with impunity without being sued.

Apart from having devastating consequences for the environment and the local communities, the impunity of illegal logging also leads to an estimated tax evasion loss of about 5-10 million USD per year.

Further instances of legal infractions without prosecution are the illegal takeover of land for sugar cane plantations through the expropriation of land belonging to Cameroonians by French multinationals, Somdiaa, and human rights violations registered at Bolloré Socapalm Plantations.

Besides, foreign companies like Bolloré, Rougier, and Elf appear to employ mercenaries of the company Africa Security Cameroon SARL, which often meet workers' protests with violence without legal consequences.

Also, France still exercises far-reaching monetary control over its former colonies in SSA. When the Euro was introduced in 1999, the CFA Franc was tied in a fixed parity to it, just like it was linked to the old French franc. Subsequently, France has continued to maintain the decision-making authority over the CFA area in Africa. According to the European Commission's agreement, it only needs to consult the Commission for far-reaching changes that will affect the entire Euro-area. Almost all decisions regarding the monetary policy of the whole CFA area cannot be taken without the approval of France.

Along the same line, the conventions stipulate conditions reaching into the internal financial policy of the Francophone countries. Also, as with the French franc, the CFA is only convertible to the Euro through the Banque de France. Therefore, the CFA franc used in Francophone West Africa and the one used in the Central African area cannot be directly exchanged into other currencies without the permission of the French Central Bank. After all, all CFA countries are obliged to deposit 65% of their monetary reserves in the French Treasury, which implies an enormous capital flight from Africa.

Political Interference

In Cameroon's presidential elections, it has been reported that President Paul Biya's campaigns were mainly sponsored by the French oil company Elf Aquitaine. In a revelation about the Elf corruption scandal, Alfred Sirven, ex-manager at Elf, revealed its involvement in financing Biya. He stated that:

"Un jour, jétais reçu à la presidence Camerounaise par le président Paul Biya. Il avait besoin de 45 million pour sa campagne. J'étais seul avec lui, ces gars-là, ils ne font confiance à personne. Ils ont besoin de cash et ils ont besoin que ce cash échappe à leur ministre des Finances. C'est pour cela que le group Elf monte des offshore qui échappent à tout contrôle, y compris au contrôle des autorités locales qu'ils ne sont pas sûrs de tenor [...]" Roughly translated as:

"One day, I was received at the Cameroonian presidency by President Paul Biya. He needed 45 million for his campaign. I was alone with him; these guys don't trust anyone. They need cash, and they need this cash to escape their finance minister's attention. This is why the Elf group sets up offshore companies that escape all control, including the control of local authorities that they are not sure of controlling."

Even after this expose, the offshore accounts operated by Elf persist. Moreover, it has been officially disclosed by Lok Le Floch-Pringent, an ex-president at Elf, that without the support of the company, Biya would probably no longer be in power.

Military Presence

France considers Cameroon as its first partner for military cooperation in sub-Saharan Africa, even though only 50 French soldiers are permanently stationed there compared to about 2900 in

Djibouti. This is likely due to the strong military-industrial relation between them that is underscored by the constant rise of the Cameroonian defence budget ($400+ million in 2018). Of course, French companies are the major contractors.

Reassessing the Imprints of Lack of Leadership Strategy in Africa

Sub-Saharan Africa's development challenges - civil wars, decrepit institutions, corruption, social disequilibrium, ethnic mistrust, and poverty are all in the public domain. They have become the subjects of several studies by economists, policymakers, and politicians alike. For example, no less a personality than the late Kofi Annan, a former UN Secretary-General and Ghanaian statesman, admitted that "for many people in other parts of the world, the mention of Africa evokes images of civil unrest, war, poverty, disease, and mounting social problems."

In recent times, a Zambian Scholar, Dambisa Moyo, posed the following pertinent questions: "Why is it that Africa alone among the continents of the world seems to be locked into a cycle of dysfunction? Why is it that out of all the continents in the world, Africa seems unable to get its foot on the economic ladder convincingly? Why, in a recent survey, did seven out of the top ten 'failed states' hail from that continent? Are Africa's people universally more incapable? Are its leaders genetically more venal, more ruthless, more corrupt? Are its policymakers more innately feckless? What is it about Africa that holds it back, that seems to render it incapable of joining the rest of the globe in the 21st Century?"

Taking the discussion further, Wangari Maathai, winner of the Nobel

Peace Prize from Kenya, expressed the views widely shared by many Africans: "One of the major tragedies of post-colonial Africa is that the African people have trusted their leaders, but only a few of those leaders have honoured that trust. What has held Africa back and continues to do so has its roots in a lack of principled, ethical, and Afrocentric leadership.

Also, Nigeria's celebrated novelist, Chinua Achebe, was emphatic in his excoriation of African leaders for the development challenges bedevilling the continent. According to him, the trouble with Nigeria (the most populous country in Africa) was simply and squarely a failure of leadership.

Because of this and other realities, it becomes important for us to examine the imprints of bad leadership in SSA.

Corruption and Poor Governance - Africa's Twin Vices

At independence, most African countries were presented with an opportunity to chart new directions in the development plan to improve the livelihoods of their people. All African states' policy agenda at independence was mainly to fight ignorance, poverty, and disease.

However, to date, most SSA countries are still experiencing low levels of development characterized by high levels of poverty, unemployment, insecurity, and moral decay. All these development challenges are partly blamed on poor governance and, more particularly, on misrule and high levels of corruption in the region.

Indeed, the case of SSA countries is one of a paradox in that although they are rich in terms of human and natural resources, they remain at the bottom of the global development index.

The grim reality in SSA can be summarized in the words of Rwekaza, who observed that 'while other regions increased in per capita income, raised literacy levels and improved healthcare, per capita income in Africa was roughly the same throughout the 1990s as it was at independence in the 1960s.'

In other words, Africa's, especially SSA's, development stagnated and declined significantly over the years, with nearly half of the continent's population living on less than a dollar a day, thus representing 30 per cent of the world's poor in the '90s and up till the 2010s. This state of affairs is mainly attributable to the culture of impunity, corruption, and lousy leadership in Africa.

To fully understand the danger posed by corruption, we only need to look at statistics obtained from reputable organizations and researchers.

According to Dreher and Herzfeld (2005), the effect of corruption on the Gross Domestic Product (GDP) growth is so huge that an increase of corruption by about one index point reduces GDP growth by 0.13 percentage points and GDP per capita by 425 USD.

In Africa, the ADB estimated that the continent loses over 300 billion USD annually through corruption. This amounts to 25 per cent of its GDP and is higher than donor aid inflow.

In the words of Kofi Annan, "Corruption undermines economic performance, weakens democratic institutions and the rule of law, disrupts social order and destroys public trust, thus allowing organized crime, terrorism and other threats to human security to flourish...And it is always the public good that suffers."

Also, Nigeria's celebrated novelist, Chinua Achebe, opined that "Without doubt, corruption has permeated the African society.

Anyone who can say that corruption in Africa has not become alarming is either a fool, a crook, or else does not live in this continent."

The effects of corruption in Africa have been devastating; one African commentator once observed that corruption and HIV/AIDS were the two major killers in the continent.

Due to the twin evils of corruption and bad governance, many African leaders have completely driven themselves away from achieving their people's aspirations and needs. They have created what is described as the 'personal rule paradigm' whereby they treat their offices as a form of personal property and a source of private gain. They openly appoint unqualified and incompetent personnel into key positions at state-owned institutions and government parastatals in other to build patronage, and at the same time, undermine development.

Table 8: Corruption in sub-Saharan Africa

Name	Country	Estimated Fortune in USD
General Sani Abacha	Nigeria	20 billion
President H. Boigny	Ivory Coast (Cote d'Ivoire)	6 billion
General Ibrahim Babangida	Nigeria	5 billion
President Mobutu Sese Seko	Zaire	4 billion
President Mousa Traore	Mali	2 billion
President Henri Bedie	Ivory Coast	300 million
President Dennis N'guesso	Congo	200 million
President Omar Bongo	Gabon	80 million
President Paul Biya	Cameroon	70 million
President Haile Mariam	Ethiopia	30 million

Extracted from Gbenga (2007)

Class Identity - Threat to Development

Numerous scholars on development studies have attributed the lack of national identity as the biggest threat to national development in African countries.

During the colonial era, nationalist leaders identified with ordinary peasants and workers. Workers' associations were very active in the struggles for independence across sub-Saharan Africa. However, this harmonious social identity has now been replaced with an "us" versus "them" mentality. "Us" may be the privileged ruling class and "them" being the poor and ordinary citizens. Similarly, the "Us" could be military officers while "them" are the civilians. Such social divisions bedevil almost all African countries.

What's more, when African leaders speak, they often talk about grandiose schemes that often benefit themselves and their cronies, with no attention paid to national development per se.

In contrast, Thomas Sankara, one of Africa's most incredible sons, showed us what can be achieved when a cohesive national identity is forged.

United as a country, Burkina Faso was able to fight corruption, disease, and poverty. In the four years he ruled (1983-87), literacy levels improved from 13 per cent to 73 per cent. The land was redistributed from the feudal landlords directly to the peasants, making the country self-sufficient in food production within three years.

He reduced the salaries of all public servants, including his own, sold off the government-owned fleet of Mercedes-Benz cars, and made the Renault 5 brand of car the official government vehicle. He also forbade first-class airline tickets for government officials on national assignments and appointed women to higher government positions. They were able to build railway lines and improve infrastructure in the country without having to borrow from international financial institutions.

That he achieved all these within a short time was not a miracle but credit to good governance and a genuine desire to create national cohesiveness and identity.

Ineffective Leadership

The raison d'etre of government is to provide good governance described by Professor Robert Rotberg as "the delivery of high-quality political goods to citizens." Political goods, he opined, include: "security and safety, the rule of law, human rights, political participation, sustainable economic opportunity, and human development."

Most African leaders have failed to meet the benchmarks listed above. The ineffectiveness of these leaders is traceable to the nature of African politics that is based on imported Eurocentric systems of government. For example, African politicians aim solely to win elections and to enjoy the perks of office. It is always a 'winner-takes-all' game in which the victorious party rarely carries the opposition along in decision-making. Policies, programs, or even ideas for governing their countries seldom form part of their scheme for attaining power. There are little or no party ideologies, no meaningful manifestoes, and candidates for elective offices often depend on money to win.

Table 9: Democratic index by region

Rank	Region	Countries	2019
1	North America	2	8.59
2	Western Europe	21	8.35
3	Latin America and the Caribbean	24	6.13
4	Asia and Australasia	28	5.67
5	Central and Eastern Europe	28	5.42
6	Sub-Saharan Africa	46	4.26
7	The Middle East and North	20	3.53

Source: Economist Intelligence Unit (EIU

Consequently, many of those elected into public offices in Africa are ominously ill-prepared to discharge duties expected of their respective offices. Some of them assume office without thinking through how they will tackle problems bedevilling their nations. According to Professor Abubakar Siddique, "some African Presidents did not have any articulate programme on the assumption of office. The programme drawn for him by some eminent technocrats and scholars is often ignored. They only follow their moods, prayers, and quirks."

More troubling is that some African leaders are completely unaware of their countries' major problems. Even after attaining power, they spend little or no time trying to develop agendas or plans for the country. Not only do they fail to improve the lot of their citizens, but they also seem unconcerned and uninterested in trying to do better. So, rather than confronting issues facing their nations, these leaders often engage in mischievously orchestrated plots to blunt populist demands for accountability and circumvent the people's will.

Also, the powers and majesty of high office have made many African leaders adopt a "know-it-all" attitude toward governance that prevents them from listening to advisers and citizens whose ideas run contrary to their own. Many African leaders are also afflicted by the debilitating political vice of arrogance that prevents them from educating and informing themselves about the challenges and dictates of high office. They substitute dictation and monologues for reasoned debates and meaningful discussions about important national issues.

As mentioned earlier, many African leaders rather see themselves as rulers who do not feel obliged to serve their people's interests. This is one of the legacies of colonial rule. The instruments of governance were taken away from the people and reposed in either the colonial officials or their hand-picked local chiefs. As a result, the leaders are more concerned with self-preservation and ethnic solidarity. Thus, they do everything to tighten their grip on power and amass wealth to sustain their expensive lifestyles and reward their cronies.

Personalism

In the presidential system of government, currently practised in many African countries, the president occupies a key position. So many citizens depend on a broad range of perks and privileges. The president has varieties of concessions, inducements, favours, and perks he bestows on his allies and supporters. He also can make life unbearable for his critics and opponents by denying them the opportunity to improve their businesses and lives.

The combination of incentives and sanctions provides a powerful impetus for citizens to seek the president's approval and to court his friendship. The president and other political office holders recognize that their ability to retain office depends on the extent to which they can satisfy their cronies, friends, and supporters. As aptly observed by Professor Collier, "patronage financed by embezzlement has been the standard means of retaining power," With special reference to leaders of many African countries. The mutually beneficial relationship between political leaders who dole out benefits to favour-seeking parasitic cronies has led to African politics' being characterized as clientelist, prebendalistic, and neo-patrimonial. Virtually all SSA governments are characterized by one key attribute - the elevation of selfish interests over public good and the national interest. Rather than using the instrument of power to improve the citizens' welfare and quality of life, many African leaders engage in cartelization of their national resources, granting concessions to their local and foreign cronies, often in ways that are inimical to the national interest.

A significant consequence of cronyism is that government jobs and most appointments are offered not on merit or competence but favouritism and patronage. Personal interests influence leadership decisions and often lead to the appointment of mediocre ones into public office.

Because loyalty trumps competence, African leaders tend to recruit underachieving underlings who can be trusted to advance the leaders' selfish agenda.

On their part, the stooges spend time propitiating the ruling class at the expense of competence and productivity. Professor Van de Wallet aptly described this situation when he wrote, "Political authority in Africa is based on the granting of favours, in an endless series of dyadic exchanges that go from the village level to the highest reaches of the central state.

For example, many African Presidents saturate their cabinet and government agencies with genuflecting cronies from their political party. These political hacks neither had nor were they ever expected to possess the requisite skills and expertise for their positions. Far too often, these obsequious party loyalists and ethnic jingoists cannot tackle governance's pressing needs.

More importantly, they lack the courage to present the President with an objective assessment of policies and programs, especially if they damage the President's image. Public servants who gave their honest opinions often had their careers possibly destroyed by votaries of the presidency.

We have seen numerous court orders disobeyed by such governments; we have also witnessed the invasion of the National Assembly Complex and even the official residence of Supreme Court judges by state security officers based on untenable reasons.

The President could do no wrong to their die-hard supporters, and they often overlook their excesses and shortcomings. This flotsam of personalization of governance has become painfully obvious. The effectiveness of government is considerably diminished, perhaps crippled, as the President operates without the creativity and ingenuity of the all-too-eager to please technocrats who sacrifice competence for the imperative of securing the President's approval.

As a result, such Presidents are given a free hand to appoint whomever he likes into public office, not minding the competence or character of the appointee. This often gives rise to lopsided appointments of directors in government agencies and parastatals. Also, such governments are fond of clamping down on critics.

It is worrisome that the core loyalists of such leaders' place support for the individual above national interest, which is one of the manifestations of leadership failure in Africa.

This situation buttressed Frank Sutton's assessment of African governments more than 30 years ago when he observed that "African governments are indeed weak and afflicted with influences that make them too often governments, not of laws, but personal authority and preference."

Lack of integration and unity

Lack of unity and economic integration among African countries is another manifestation of shallow strategic thinking among African leaders in charge of the countries' internal and external policies. Here, I shall discuss the lack of integration and cooperation among African leaders by highlighting the variability of trade among countries in Africa. The focus is on Ghana and Nigeria (the two largest economies in ECOWAS). This lack of unity among African leaders can be seen in the disintegration of West African markets, as shown in **Tables 10-13**

No	Destination	Value of exports in US Dollars (millions)	No	Country	Value of imports in US dollars (millions)
1	China	2800	1	China	1890
2	Switzerland	2460	2	USA	976
3	India	2380	3	UK	685
4	South Africa	1970	4	India	582
5	Netherlands	966	5	Belgium	532
6	UAE	899	6	Turkey	466
7	USA	704	7	South Africa	357
8	UK	415	8	Vietnam	316
9	France	377	9	UAE	275
10	Italy	308	10	Canada	266

Table 10: Ghana's Top 10 Exports and Imports Partners 2019.

Source: Comtrade, 2020

No	Destination	Value of exports in US dollars (billions)	No	Country	Value of imports in US dollars (billions)
1	India	8.3	1	China	12.0
2	Spain	5.3	2	India	5.7
3	Netherlands	4.9	3	USA	4.67
4	Ghana	4.0	4	Netherlands	3.49
5	France	3.6	5	Belgium	2.37
6	South Africa	3.2	6	Swaziland	1.55
7	United States	2.8	7	Germany	1.45
8	Italy	2.1	8	UK	1.34
9	China	1.7	9	UAE	1.19
10	Indonesia	1.5	10	South Korea	1.01

Table 11: Nigeria's Top 10 Exports and Imports Partners 2019.
Source: Comtrade, 2020

No	Destination	Value of exports in US dollars (billions)	No	Country	Value of imports in US dollars (billions)
1	USA	73	1	Germany	88
2	Germany	46	2	USA	67
3	France	31	3	China	65
4	Netherlands	30	4	Netherlands	53
5	China	30	5	France	38
6	Ireland	27	6	Belgium	32
7	Belgium	16.4	7	Italy	26
8	Switzerland	15.6	8	Switzerland	23
9	Spain	13.6	9	Spain	21
10	Italy	12.7	10	Norway	19.7

Table 12: UK's Top 10 Exports and Imports Partners 2019.
Source: Comtrade, 2020

No	Destination	Value of exports in US dollars (billions)	No	Country	Value of imports in US dollars (billions)
1	USA	133	1	China	124
2	Fracne	119	2	Netherlands	98
3	China	108	3	USA	81
4	Netherlands	92	4	France	73
5	UK	88	5	France	64
6	Italy	76	6	Poland	64
7	Poland	73	7	Italy	53
8	Austria	71	8	Czech Republic	53
9	Switzerland	64	9	Austria	46
10	Belgium	51	10	Belgium	45

Table 13: Germany's Top 10 Exports and Imports Partners 2019.
Source: Comtrade, 2020

As shown in **Table 8** above, which displays Ghana's main export partners, no member of ECOWAS features in the top ten list. In the list, South Africa, a fellow African country, represents $1.9 billion in exports, whereas China, Switzerland, and India (non-African countries) represent at least $2 billion of trade. Further, the remaining are Western countries.

As far as import is concerned, **Table 10** does not reveal any evidence of integration between Ghana and other members of ECOWAS or other sub-Saharan countries. China is the topmost import partner, and its share largely surpasses any other country's share. Additionally, except for South Africa, no other country in West Africa features on the table. One can even argue that South Africa has become a major trading partner with Ghana because of its status as one of Africa's two largest economies. As such, their deals are negotiated on a bilateral basis and not through any continental association.

One would expect that flow of trade within ECOWAS member countries would exceed trade flows between ECOWAS countries and non-members of ECOWAS. However, the trade statistics in **Table 11** show that in the year 2019, forty-three years after the creation of ECOWAS, the top three destinations of Nigeria's products are not members of ECOWAS (India, Spain, and the Netherlands). Also, except for one country (Ghana, a neighbouring economy), none of Nigeria's major export destinations is a member of ECOWAS. A check on the country's import trade index reveals an even more disintegrated image of the Community. The statistics in **Table 11,** which depicts Nigeria's import partners, show that none of Nigeria's top 10 markets is part of the ECOWAS zone. China occupies the top position, and the UK, Nigeria's former colonial master, is also on the list. And only one African country (Swaziland) features on the list. The data symbolizes the failure of African leaders to promote trade among their countries.

These cases from ECOWAS members reveal an absence of integration in the trade variable within sub-Saharan Africa. The two countries examined (Ghana and Nigeria) share common characteristics: they are African countries, former colonies with similar colonial experiences, and their main area of business is outside the scope of Africa.

In contrast, **Tables 11 and 12** indicate a great degree of integration in European countries' economies, as shown in the trade figures posted for the UK and Germany in the same year - 2019. For instance, apart from China and the USA (the world's two largest economies), other countries on the exports and imports lists for both countries feature only other European countries such as Belgium, Italy, and the Netherlands.

These findings are consistent with previous studies on trade within SSA and Europe. David J. Francis revealed that African countries' export was directed mainly towards the West's industrial countries and some to Asia. Industrial countries and Asia, he said, took up about 80 per cent of the continent's GDP.

While any variables that have been considered in this book could lend themselves to alternate explanations, the most significant stumbling block to integration in West Africa, in particular, seems to be the divide between Anglophone/Francophone leadership. It can be seen that the French-speaking leaders in Africa, through a series of treaties of cooperation with Metropolitan France, and the formation of such organizations as Conseil de l'Entente (Entente Council), OCAM, and numerous others sought to cohere under virtual French leadership. The solidarity among those French African states has somehow widened the gulf between French and English-speaking countries that often see themselves as rivals in matters they ought to cooperate.

In West Africa, scholars have argued that this attitude is dictated by the Francophone leadership's attempt to counter Nigeria's hegemony. For instance, Adibe noted that Nigeria is perceived as a hegemonic threat by her Francophone neighbours. This misconception constitutes an impediment to the success of ECOWAS in integrating the sub-region.

Suffice to say that the same arguments can be made about other parts of sub-Saharan Africa, including Southern Africa (Southern Africa Development Commission), East Africa (East Africa Community), and Central Africa (Economic Community of Central Africa States).

From these perspectives, the responsibility to promote cooperation and integration and to establish an economic union in Africa is a way of raising the living standards of their people and to maintain and enhance economic stability through a secure Africa; however, it is sad to say African leaders have been unsuccessful. Today, Africa is only slightly more secure and economically more integrated than it was about 30 years ago.

However, I want to mention that the present crop of African leaders can achieve more if they act collectively and decisively in cooperative efforts to diversify their economies and engage in technological development, as well as in manufacturing and trading among themselves, and resolving conflicts within the continent.

Conclusion

So far, this chapter has unearthed many facts about Western leadership orientation and the reasons why this may not be suitable to the African setting. The readers can also clearly see why the wholesale adoption of these foreign ideas amounts to foolishness on the part of African leaders. Moreover, it offers an excellent view of the pitfalls of shallow strategies by leaders of SSA and briefly discussed how these narcissistic leaders had undermined their nations' March to development. The examples of African leaders who got caught in its web should be seen as cautionary tales, reminding us that every nation needs checks and balances against the abuse of power. Without these safeguards, any leader, no matter how enlightened, can descend into the cesspit of despotic rule.

In essence, the chapter has succeeded in laying the foundation for why Africans must look inwards for solutions to the myriad of challenges confronting them. After all, no one can love Africa more than herself. The philosophy underpinning this thinking shall be the focus of the next chapter.

7

AFROCENTRIC LEADERSHIP: ISSUES, TRENDS AND PROSPECTS

Chapter 7

African economic psychology is generally characterized by powerful connections between objects, humans, and the supernatural. Although the emphasis put on each of these elements and the interrelationships among them can vary from one ethnic group or tribe to another, the quest for equilibrium with other human beings and with the supernatural is the guiding principle ... Self-reliance and self-interest tend to take a backseat to ethnicity and group loyalty –

(Dia, 1994, p. 176)

As with the West and Asia, it is unrealistic to suggest that what can be said about leadership applies across the whole of sub-Saharan Africa. Given the cultural heterogeneity of most African countries, similar dangers exist with individual countries. Notwithstanding, there are still sufficient similarities among African cultures from a tentative African leadership model that can be drawn. In this chapter, we shall consider an alternative to the Western notion of leadership known as the Afrocentric leadership theory. What does it mean for a leadership structure to be Afrocentric, and are there possibilities of having a better leadership orientation in Africa if Afrocentric leadership ideas are imbibed?

The Case for African-centred Leadership Perspective

In Africa, individual achievements are much less valued than inter-communal relations. The value of economic transactions lies more in the ritual surrounding them and their capacity to enhance group ties. Wealth is first extended family or clan wealth, and second tribal wealth. In many instances, rituals, ceremonies, allocation of scant resources to clan affiliates, reciprocity, and interpersonal relations are natural responsibilities of leadership in African cultures.

African societies tend to be egalitarian within age groups but hierarchical between age groups. As a result, leaders usually behave and are expected to behave paternalistically. Leaders bestow favour and expect obeisance from their followers. Consensus is highly valued, and the decision-making process within age-grade levels can therefore take considerable time. Between social levels (downwards), observance of hierarchy means that consensus can be achieved relatively faster.

African cultures also tend to have a great capacity for tolerance and forgiveness. Or how else can we explain the various attempts at reconciliation with former oppressors by African leaders like Nelson Mandela, Jomo Kenyatta, Shehu Shagari, and Julius Nyerere?

Many observers continue to wonder at this remarkable capacity to forgive and forget past misdeeds. Nelson Mandela epitomizes this image of a tolerant leader. He came out of three decades of persecution and imprisonment to become the architect of Black/White reconciliation in South Africa. Where else but Africa can one find this sort of thing?

However, such tolerance runs counter to Western market philosophies, which espouses the Darwinist Theory of 'Survival of the Fittest.' In the current paradigm, it is the leader's job to eliminate poor performers in an organization. The hard-faced managerial disposition currently employed in most international organizations, with its macho triumphalist tone, is quite revealing. For instance, existing Western management theories suggest that managerial success is to be measured in terms of the magnitude of workforce cuts achieved: organizations are supposed to be 'lean' and 'mean.' When such leadership rhetoric addresses the willingness to accept mistakes that include the caveat of swift retribution if mistakes persist or are not more than compensated for by successes.

When African management practices are compared to Western models, many scholars have wrongly stated, inadvertently perhaps, that there is an acute shortage of quality leadership and management in Africa. The crux of the matter here is that such views misconstrue the potential impacts of African leadership orientation and wrongly conclude that greater congruence with Western frameworks is always needed.

In many African societies, greater emphasis is placed on a leader's ability to honour their obligations to ethnic affiliates without necessarily denying others. Thus, it is expected that an organization will not flounder because of ethnic cleavages. As outlined in the Western model, vision may therefore be out of place in many African organizations. Debates concerning whether or not transformational leadership is practised in the West makes its adoption in Africa even more tenuous.

African Leadership Framework

The fundamental African leadership framework is seen in the theory of Afrocentrism. The main thrust of this theory is the centrality and supremacy of African culture and knowledge for solving African development challenges. Afrocentrism is a scientific effort towards African development based on African history, culture, behavioural patterns, beliefs, and norms. It is not an imitation of Western leadership models. Afrocentrism is African-centred research on indigenous African cultures as a way of harvesting a variety of leadership principles, patterns, practices, institutions, ceremonies, and ideas for contemporary use.

The history of Afrocentrism can be traced to the works of eminent scholars and activists like W.E.B. Du Bois, Marcus Garvey, Cheikh Anta Diop, Malcolm X, George James, and many others. They tried to understand the world from the perspectives of African cultural values. However, Afrocentrism as a theoretical approach to research in the social sciences has been attributed to Molefi Asante's monumental work published in 1980 titled: "Afrocentricity: The Theory of Social Change." He described Afrocentricity as a framework of reference where a given phenomenon about Africa is viewed through the lens of the peoples of Africa. Afrocentrism shows that just like the Western and Oriental cultures, Africans also have their ideas, norms, traditions, culture, and values that influence their worldview. Further, Afrocentrists argue that Afrocentricity remains the most appropriate paradigm to apply when discussing Africa's issues— whether political or otherwise—because it places Africa at the centre of such discussions and analysis.

Afrocentrism is a direct response to Eurocentrism - a cultural phenomenon that places European cultural values as superior to other cultures and universalizes European, and by extension, American experiences, for other cultures in the world. Eurocentrism is a subset of Western imperialism, and it views the realities of non-

Western societies from Western prism and advocates for the broad imitation of a Western leadership model based on Western values - democracy, equality, free markets, human rights, individuality, social justice, and secularity as a panacea for all kinds of development challenges, regardless of the historical and cultural differences of all societies across the world. European colonization of Africa involved the widespread exploitation of the region and the imposition of European culture, which contributed to the displacement of traditional African leadership institutions and structures. Consequently, even after independence, African countries adopted Western development theories such as neo-liberalism and modernization theories which have failed to achieve the desired objectives.

Afrocentrism argues that Western leadership and its development theories are based on European culture and norms. Given that African experience greatly differs from that of America or Europe, Afrocentrism posits that using Western theories to explain African people's ethos is inappropriate.

Assumptions of Afrocentrism

The theoretical basis of Afrocentrism is rooted in the core cultural characteristics of African societies. The principle of Afrocentrism postulates that culture matters a lot in the orientation to centeredness. It is also important in providing the lenses with which one views and understands societal realities, and in this instance, African societies. The theory of Afrocentrism proposes four major theoretical assumptions about human beings:

- The collective conceptualization of human beings;

- The spiritual nature of human beings;

- The effective approach to knowledge; and

- The interconnectedness of all beings in the universe

Afrocentrism conceives individual identity as a collective identity, and a person is then considered an integral part of society. An African adage aptly portrays this philosophy, "I am because we are, and because we are, I am." Ensuing this assumption of collective identity are two other principles of *"humanness"* and *"communication."*

Afrocentrists present the idea of humanness in Africa as MAAT. Simply put, MAAT means conduct, morals, and customs. MAAT has been identified as a natural law because it has corresponding meanings in all African societies. In southwest Nigeria, MAAT is known as "omoluwabism," while in southern Africa, it is called "Ubuntu."

The moral principles of MAAT are fundamental to African culture, and they constitute the bedrock of the society in regulating socio-political behaviour for the attainment of good governance and development. The prevailing moral standards of individuals in society determine the quality of governance since individuals run the government.

Afrocentrism also proposes that the spiritual aspect of African life is as real as the material component. This idea of spirituality explains why religion plays an important role in African culture. Concerning governance, religion is a cultural phenomenon that was a source of political legitimacy in precolonial Africa. Moreover, spirituality relates to the African belief in the affective approach, which involves intuition, emotions, and reason. Effective emotions and logical reasoning would help in the immediate attainment of the truth rather than through a step-by-step logic. Besides, intuition plays a crucial role in pre-colonial African life.

Analysing governance issues and leadership with Afrocentric leadership theories may seem unusual; however, it is an appropriate principle that Africans should imbibe if they intend to catch up with the West or the Asian Tigers. Since Western leadership theories are based on Western experience and promote Western interests, Africans require a theoretical framework based on African values and one that promotes African interests.

In this context, Afrocentrism remains the only theory in which the centrality of African values, perceptions, leadership principles, and interests predominate. The theory allows scholars to place the historical experience, side-by-side with culture, as the central theme to analysing leadership, governance, and development in Africa.

The Afrocentric assumption of leadership does challenge orthodox Western assumptions about competition, individualism, materialism, and rationality, which form the foundations of many Western leadership theories. The failure of Western leadership theories to achieve development in sub-Saharan Africa calls for the development of indigenous theories directly linked to African experiences rather than Western realities.

Afrocentrism aims at correcting the disparaging distortions of African people's contributions, histories, and achievements to civilization perpetuated through centuries of Western propaganda. In this regard, Afrocentrism argues that the major reason poverty and underdevelopment persist in sub-Saharan Africa is a direct consequence of blurry Western perspectives and its misplaced benchmarks on Africans. Therefore, Africa's problems cannot be delinked from centuries of cultural degradation and economic exploitation perpetrated by Western hegemony. For close to 300 years, the African continent was subjugated by the Europeans, and the Arabs to a lesser extent, first through the slave trade and later colonization. Through the capitalist global trading system, the West's exploitation of Africa has continued apace. Examples include the EU and USA subsidization of their Agricultural sectors to the tune of approximately €48 billion and $20 billion respectively on an annual basis. Meanwhile, poor African countries are coerced to remove all subsidies and other trade restrictions on agriculture as recommended by the World Trade Organization (WTO) and the International Monetary Fund (IMF). Consequently, farmers in Africa cannot produce competitively, and, as a result, many of them have been driven out of the market.

Given this condition, solving Africa's problems is mainly the lack of leadership ideals to ensure that the region's economic interests are protected. The challenge of governance in Africa is due to the lack of leaders who are culturally inclined to pursue African interests in the face of Western imperialism. Therefore, any intervention concerning leadership issues in Africa should be guided by the fundamental question, 'is this in Africa's interest?' This same question should guide any governance, leadership, or management reform to be adopted in sub-Saharan Africa.

Afrocentric Theories of Governance

There are many Afrocentric theories of leadership and good governance. These Afrocentric principles, some of which have been identified, are appropriate for applying Afrocentric theories of leadership for achieving long-term development goals. The Afrocentric theories of leadership require that African interests must guide governance and decision-making processes in the region. Thus, the psychological outlook and actions of political leadership should primarily advance the interest of a country. Political interest should also be geared towards promoting communal consciousness in the people. In this context, collective consciousness is the objective of a group of people uniting to achieve a common objective, and it signals a full commitment to a group's vision.

Therefore, a requisite condition for any society to achieve its vision is the total commitment and cooperation between the leaders and followers. However, the responsibility to mobilize popular participation in decision-making rests squarely on the shoulders of the leaders because any political reform that is not based on popular participation cannot last long.

Afrocentric theories of governance insist that any effective leadership system which will guarantee good governance must have such characteristics as:

- Purposefulness;

- Benevolence;

- History-consciousness;

- Communicative;

- Concordant; and

- Populist.

It can be seen that the proponents of Afrocentric theories of governance are not calling for the reinstitution of indigenous governance systems for contemporary African societies. Instead, we are advocating adopting the good governance qualities of Afrocentrism and its modification to reflect current African situations since those qualities are already part of the African experience. Let us now closely examine the characteristics of effective leadership in governance as articulated by Afrocentrism.

Purposefulness

A purposeful African leadership in a political system is a legitimately instituted, representative government. It is imbued with a national vision and the capacity to actualize this vision. The capacity to effectively implement policies depends on several factors, including the information available to the leaders, the economic resources available, the respect which citizens have for the government, and the constitutional provisions for policy formulation. The mass media, the public service, the intelligence service, the armed forces, the public force, and the civil society organizations (CSOs) are essential instruments that leaders can use to realize their objectives.

Benevolence

According to Afrocentric theorists, benevolent leadership is one in which the political leaders are both willing and dedicated to pursuing the general welfare of the people. In this instance, the political elite is the assemblage of leaders of the major ethnic, professional, religious, and social groups. It is their responsibility to redirect the rest of the nation along with the national goals. This means that governance is not all about the elected representatives alone and other stakeholders steering one government agency or the other.

As discussed earlier, this benevolent spirit will revive the African communal spirit of collective identity and responsibility. For multi-ethnic countries like Cameroon, Ghana, and Nigeria, the concern is that collective identity may be threatened by the diversity of ethnic groups. Nevertheless, researches have shown that structural commonalities exist among the ethnic groups in these countries, which can be built upon to achieve collective identity.

History-consciousness

African political leaders must manifest a consciousness of African history that has been relegated by years of Western imperialism. African leaders must be conscious of Africa's role in world history and its place in the current global scheme of things. African leaders who lack such attributes will only repeat the mistakes of the past.

Due to the imperialism of Western epistemology, which has entrenched the notion that nothing good can come from Africa, the African development agenda has always been based on Western ideas. Consequently, the region remains dependent on Western ideology and has seemed a liability to human history. To reverse this trend, imbibing the consciousness of African experiences is important to make African leaders believe in themselves and begin to embrace indigenous cultural knowledge for combating Africa's lingering challenges.

Communicative

Communicative leadership is committed to sharing information with the governed freely. This keeps the populace adequately informed about government policies. For communication to be effective, the leadership must employ a language understandable to the people. The communicative leadership system will also adopt a philosophical outlook (constitution, manifesto, principles, and morals) acceptable to the masses.

Concordant

This quality deals with the ability of leadership to advance consensus politics. Afrocentric theories have identified three factors necessary for achieving concordance in a political system. First is the ability of leaders to forge a consensus for policy formulation and implementation. Second is the existence of an effective apparatus for resolving disputes and enforcing discipline within the ranks of the leaders. The third is the leaders' consciousness of the collective nature of their responsibilities. Even when consensus does not exist on a particular issue, the leadership cadre must command the support of the majority of its members over such a policy to ensure acceptability and success.

Populist

African leaders must ensure the popular participation of the citizenry in the policy formulation and implementation processes. In an Afrocentric political system, decision-making should be democratized in such a way as to involve the grassroots, local, and national levels.

Thus, policy formulation and implementation should be through representative organs of government and public involvement. The rights of women should also be entrenched for popular participation in the governance of African societies. All barriers to female participation in government rooted in religion or tradition should be dismantled entirely.

However, it must be pointed out that these Afrocentric theories of governance are not so different from the mainstream principles of good governance espoused by Western scholars, including accountability, participation, legitimacy, transparency, and predictability. However, even though these mainstream principles of governance are desirable for their universal applicability, the practical implementation of these principles is submerged in implementing imperialist political system models like Western liberal democracy and neo-liberalism, which have had devastating effects on sub-Saharan Africa. Therefore, Africans should look inward and develop home-grown effective leadership principles based on their cultural experiences.

Afrocentrism versus Western Belief

Afrocentrism has its roots in the culture, experiences, and values held by Africans before the advent of colonialism. It cannot be denied that centuries of Western imperialism badly affected Africa and suppressed its philosophy to the extent that Western concepts now define African lives and values.

However, African cultural heritage has been a source of guidance for African societies in conflict, peace, death, and life. At its best, it has been the basis of identity, self-confidence, and respect for the people. It also provides the foundation for leadership, decision-making, problem-solving, and hope for the present and the future.

As mentioned earlier, Afrocentric leadership theory can be summed up by the concept of MAAT or Omoluwabism or Ubuntu as it is known in different African cultures. MAAT is an African worldview that captures the essence of existence as human beings. It must again be noted that many of the cultural practices of leadership development in sub-Saharan Africa are more similar than they are different from one another.

MAAT is built on these five conceptual frameworks:

• Participatory decision making;

• Collective ownership of challenges, opportunities, and responsibilities;

• The importance of relationships over things;

• Reconciliation as a goal of conflict management; and

• Patriotism.

The positive aspects of these principles shall be discussed in turn and then applied to our leadership discourse. This is not to say that there are no negative elements of MAAT. Some of these negative aspects arose from the fact that the MAAT principles were practised mainly at communal levels and in stable environments. Part of the challenge that the proposed Afrocentric model may face is how it will transcend this predictable context. This has resulted in questions being asked about the existing practice of MAAT since:

• Loyalty to kinship may develop into ethnicity;

• Respect for elders may lead to blind loyalty to retrogressive ideas;

- Fear of the unknown may encourage primitive accumulation;

- The belief in divine kingship may encourage sit-tight rulers;

- Values attached to human relationships at the expense of personal progress may encourage wasteful spending on ceremonies; and

- Radical changes in response to rapidly changing environments may be delayed due to the desire for continuity.

To compound these problems, the current trend towards globalization implicitly foregrounds Western values and can give the impression that indigenous practices are somehow inferior. The low self-esteem that results from this has caused many people in Africa to abandon their values and embrace those from the West.

Unfortunately, the negative elements of MAAT have in the past been blown out of proportion, which resulted in throwing the baby away with the bathwater. To redress this imbalance, we shall explore the positive elements of MAAT's five principles and how they could be applied to leadership issues in sub-Saharan Africa

1. Participatory Decision-making

At first glance, indigenous African leadership seems autocratic. However, the people or their representatives' approval was still critical for the legitimacy of leaders, as shown by the various cultures discussed in Chapter 3. The accountability of African leaders was reinforced because there were many potential candidates for leadership. So, strict criteria were used to select leaders at that time. Again, the decision was usually subjected to people's approval. Most

African leaders had to show competence in:

- Understanding human nature;

- Understanding human relationships;

- Diplomacy;

- Strategic thinking

- The art of war.

Therefore, African leadership was much more participatory than it appeared to outsiders. For example, among the Bantus of Southern Africa, a council of elders play a key role in governance in the following ways:

- Advising the king

- Custodianship of the kingdom

- Managing disputes on behalf of the king

- Managing leadership succession

- Proposing new laws

- Installing and dethroning kings

2. Collective Ownership of Challenges, Opportunities, and Responsibilities

Indigenous African societies believed in the principle of collective responsibility. Children were taken as children of the community rather than belonging to their parents alone. Consequently, any adult in the community could discipline an errant child at any time. Also, children were taught to respect their elders the same way that they respected their parents. Cooperation at work was greatly encouraged, and age groups would take turns working on the farms of members. A small candle loses nothing by lighting another candle: people were not expected to be jealous of the good fortune of others. In unity, ants can carry a dead elephant to their anthill: each individual was expected to play their role towards the community's well-being, according to their age, ability, experience, knowledge, and skills. Only the old, the infirm, and the very young were exempted from community tasks.

3. The Importance of Relationships Over Things

In indigenous African societies, relationships were a top priority. Uncles were fathers. Aunts were ranked the same as Mothers. Cousins or nephews were brothers or sisters. Elders in the community were seen as their parents.

The closeness of community was the beginning of African education and socialization. Family relationships were defined by shared responsibilities and values, such as seen when parents die, family members would adopt their young children. Also, cohorts that underwent initiation ceremonies would become brothers and sisters for life - the filial bond was as strong as blood relationships or ties.

4. Reconciliation as the Goal of Conflict Management

The African principles of conflict management were based on the values of fairness, trust, and reconciliation. Conflict mediation and the maintenance of human relationships were critical roles of the king and the council of chiefs.

In conflict management, the council made decisions through consensus, while the king would make the judgement after considering the position of the chiefs. The concept of openness was an important value in African courts since members of the public were allowed to attend hearings. So, disputes were managed systematically through a hierarchy of levels. Minor disputes were resolved at the level and transits to higher levels through appeal if the parties were unsatisfied with the outcome.

At the family units, elders were responsible for resolving disputes. At higher levels, chiefs would take over. The gravity of the conflict determined the level at which it would be resolved. Therefore, only big cases would be taken to the king's or the queen's court. In this setting, the goal of conflict resolution was taken as reconciliation, and peace was often maintained through the principles of inclusivity and a sense of shared heritage among the people.

It is important to note that the principles of MAAT do not solely belong to Africa's past. Up till today, many African communities still apply these principles in issues requiring collective responsibility like child care and burials. African people still see the children of their brothers and sisters as their children, and the whole family contributes towards the burial ceremonies of deceased ones.

5. Patriotism

In indigenous African cultures, collective interest often trumped personal interest. The reigns of kings, however loved or hated, were not more important than the well-being of the kingdom itself. In many cases, kings were asked to commit suicide when they lost their people's confidence.

The people understood the need for a strong security bond; they would close ranks to surmount challenges facing the community. Great emphasis was placed on group loyalty, and each child was taught their origins and history and was encouraged to see their relatives as their family members. People were continually reminded to respect their identity and not abandon their cultural values no matter the situation.

Application of Afrocentric Leadership Principles to Contemporary Issues

Previous sections have highlighted key principles of Afrocentric leadership and the processes involved in its emergence. There are many aspects of its development that are worth grafting into current leadership development initiatives in Africa. Now, let us look at how the five principles of MAAT could be positively applied to leadership development initiatives in the current era for greater effectiveness and growth.

* Participatory Leadership

As with African community leaders in the past, elections or appointments to leadership positions should be conducted with accountability and transparency. The process of leadership selection must leave followers and stakeholders satisfied as to its fairness and even-handedness.

An initiation ceremony for new leaders might be organized for new leaders to help them align with the aspirations and expectations of the people or employees in the organization. Such an orientation process could involve letting people ask the new leader pertinent questions on issues concerning the community/organization and how their leadership would make a difference.

Besides, leadership development needs to emphasize the importance of involving all stakeholders in addressing the community or organization's challenges through group projects and open participation. When people participate meaningfully in a group project, they are more likely to help take ownership of the project and success achieved. This will enhance their sense of belongingness and camaraderie.

Going forward, too much power should not be invested in individual leaders. The important role of the council of chiefs or elders to checkmate this power should be developed within a country's or an organization's leadership framework. This should be done primarily by ensuring that the community or organizations formulate effective policies and procedures, which must be strictly adhered to by all regardless of class or status.

* Collective responsibility

Taking collective responsibility is crucial to the overall success of any community or organization. In many organizations, leaders and followers play the blame game, thereby abdicating their responsibilities. The truth is that blaming others for organizational challenges could be a time-waster, diminishes the organization's ability to overcome challenges bedevilling the organization.

Collective responsibility also applies to the fair distribution of benefits or tasks. People must feel that their colleagues and everyone are contributing in equal measure to realising organizational goals and objectives and just parasites. Otherwise, they may reduce their efforts or quit. Such a situation would affect the hardworking and innovative spirit of the organization.

* Importance of relationships

MAAT's emphasis on human relationships can be successfully applied to leadership development. Organizations may be viewed as extended families, in the cultural sense, in which relationships are close-knit enough to go beyond the professional level. In contrast, Western organizations do not tend to interfere with people's personal lives outside the workplace, although what is done or experienced outside the office often affects productivity and the overall health of the organization.

As seen in Asia, African organizations may create an organizational environment where stakeholders feel close to one another and contribute to other people's lives if they perceive that would ultimately benefit the organization.

* Reconciliation

The African organizational mechanisms for conflict resolution need to ensure fairness, trust, and reconciliation as the goal. People should be free to appeal to higher authorities if they are dissatisfied with the conflict mediation/resolution process.

The main aim of conflict resolution must be relationship building by helping the people involved reach a consensus agreement in fairness to both parties. Receiving and giving forgiveness should be seen as the foundation of human relationships.

Conflicts involving a superior and a subordinate should be handled with care to balance fairness and retain respect if the senior party is in the wrong.

Leaders should delegate conflict management to others over minor issues and encourage people to resolve their conflicts at the lower levels on amicable terms. This will give top leaders more space and time to concentrate on strategic and weightier issues.

* Patriotism

The MAAT concept of patriotism simply means that organizational interests must supersede personal interests. Leadership should be ready to sacrifice short-term self-interests for long-term organizational interests. Additionally, leadership must be seen as an opportunity to serve the people rather than as a means of wielding power or accumulating wealth.

Organizations should inculcate in their staff a culture of pride in the organization. In many organizations, nowadays, the staff are made to feel that there are better organizations out there, and they seldom contribute their best. A genuine commitment to an organization depends on people consciously linking their values to the organization's values. So, it is imperative to identify these personal values and connect them to the organization's culture. Leadership development programmes like coaching, mentoring, and succession planning should emphasize the cultivation of values. One way of doing this involves adopting rituals from the African cultural context. Such rituals symbolizing success, celebration, growth, or losses will connect people and their cultural lives.

So far, we have discussed the principles of leadership as developed in indigenous African societies. It is now important to discuss how the concept of Afrocentric leadership was developed and then draw valuable lessons for its application in the current era.

Afrocentric leadership development recognizes the importance of communal benefits over personal achievements. The method for developing leadership, in this context, was through education and learning. Professor Michongwe defined African education as the ability to use what one has collected through a learning process to develop oneself and one's community or country. He further noted that modern or Western education, including most leadership development programmes, emphasizes developing oneself and not one's community. If leadership development initiatives are to be effective, they must be aimed at developing individuals and their organizations. Many of such initiatives, packaged by consultants as leadership training courses, rarely impact the organization beyond the individual level.

Lessons for Leadership Development in Africa

Effective leadership is imperative in post-colonial Africa. However, there is a dearth of leadership development models that can effectively address the need for values-based leadership, motivating Africans to transform at both personal and organizational levels. The MAAT leadership model based on African cultural practices could be helpful in this context. The main challenge is how to bring this model to the forefront of current leadership discourse.

Many valuable lessons are already emerging from an understanding of Afrocentric leadership, as presented earlier. Some requisites for existing leadership development initiatives to be effectively grafted onto African culture include:

- Adopting an experiential approach - This involves apprenticeship, coaching, and mentoring.

- Inculcation of values - leadership development programmes must be geared towards transforming lives in the affective (values) domain.

- Use of ceremonies, proverbs, and rituals - the leadership development process must include traditions and ways to connect new leaders with the people in an organization.

- Taking leadership development as a life-long process - leadership development processes should be long-term and life-long to enable leaders to adapt to change effectively.

- Planning for leadership succession in advance - African organizations must have concrete plans for leadership succession with an effective system for identifying new leaders. This will ensure a smooth transition from one leader to the next.

- Involvement of all stakeholders in leadership development planning - organizations must involve the entire board to ensure everybody is carried along and the process is fair.

- Taking leadership role as a call to serve - leadership development programmes must empower people to take the training lessons beyond the classroom. These lessons should emphasize that leadership is a call to serve.

Implications of Afrocentric Leadership for Organizations

What would an organization look like if it were to be guided by Afrocentric leadership principles? For instance, what would the organization aim to achieve, whom would it consider to be stakeholders, and how would decisions be made? We intend to answer these questions and more by drawing contrasts with typical Western leadership principles.

What is the Aim of an Organization?

Goal pursuit differs from prizing communion, as per Kantian orientation. It is also different from desire-satisfaction as per utilitarianism. All these are typically Western ideas of what ought to be the aim of a firm or a large organization with a substantial public influence. Rather than positioning an organization to satisfy variable demand, an organization led by Afrocentric values would do whatever is expected to enable its customers to live better lives objectively in terms of morality.

This orientation towards meeting people's needs means that stakeholders must regularly reflect on whether an organization is producing and selling goods or services suitable for its customers/consumers. For example, if Afrocentric leadership takes over a company that sells tobacco, they would try to shift production to something that would not cause serious bodily harm to their consumers.

In terms of what an organization should aim for, the Afrocentric approach to leadership presupposes that each person possesses noble virtues and can commune with others and be communed with. This translates into treating every person that comes in contact with it with uttermost respect because every leader must strive to meet the needs of those it is serving.

How Should Organizations Determine What Policies to Adopt?

Here, Afrocentrism differs markedly from Western principles of leadership. Typical Western scholars, appealing to Lockean (or Kantian) ideas, consider consent to be sufficient enough to give directors or managers the authority to make decisions for an organization. The fact that employees signed a contract to submit their labour-power to the direction of the business managers in exchange for a salary should be enough to warrant their obedience to managerial directives.

Of course, this approach recommends regular consultations with the workers to further the ends of a business. However, this idea does not entail authorization from employers to give their employees whatever is due to them.

In contrast, Afrocentric leadership does. Perhaps the most salient theme of the traditional African leadership approach is that leadership ought to deploy consensual democracy when making decisions. By this approach, neither consultations with employees nor the idea of giving them a vote in the decision-making process are not enough. s. Instead, everyone in the organization must agree to the essentials before moving ahead. This does not imply that everyone within the organization must share or hold similar opinions on any issue, but rather that no one should object to the proposal or hold back the rest of the team from acting on such a proposal.

How Should Conflicts Be Resolved in an Organization?

Let us consider one possible way of dealing with conflicts in the workplace as espoused by Afrocentrists. To start with, note that Western managers are known for having the discretion to dismiss an employee for a misdemeanour or underperformance. At the end of the 20th Century, for example, two-thirds of American employees were liable to be fired immediately for failing to perform, or even for no just cause - an orientation that is consistent with the contractual ethical approach; and it is worth considering what would be wrong with this act from an Afrocentric perspective.

There is something fundamentally abhorrent about immediately sacking someone perceived to be a problem in the workplace: exclusion. In contrast, inclusion is a recurring theme in Afrocentric leadership orientation. It highlights using emotional intelligence to address conflict, develop weak employees, and enable everybody to feel part of a community. Conspicuously absent from traditional African thought about leadership are ideas of using intimidation, fear, or outright dismissal without trying to bring the employee up to speed.

Moreover, a focus on community provides a good explanation of why inclusiveness should be a good leader's overarching approach. Suppose the most important thing about human societies is our capacity to commune and be communed with. In that case, a special value should encourage us to create relationships and repair them when they break down. Therefore, a leader should always ascertain why an employee erred and consider whether they could be given a second chance, rather than summarily dismissing such an employee.

How Should the Workplace Be Organized?

In the contemporary business world, efficiency is sought through managerialism, which is based on Western ideas. To minimize inputs and maximize outputs, employees are steered with money, power, and other incentives that warrant the production of standardized outputs according to particular metrics. Such an approach is justified philosophically by the idea that workers have freely accepted managerialism or that it would benefit society at large. In contrast, Afrocentric leadership is ambivalent about the effectiveness of such a mode of production.

On the one hand, managerialism is antisocial when it comes to how managers treat their subordinates. It hardly engenders or fosters a sense of belongingness among workers. Its use of steering mechanisms such as punitive threats and financial incentives is prima facie incompatible with collective participation on the part of employees. Although employees might be handsomely rewarded for doing well by managerialism criteria, yet their well-being is of little interest beyond safety considerations. Also, managerialism does not foster sympathy, rather it encourages managers to see their workers as mere production tools rather than as human beings whose interests matter in the overall scheme of things.

Additionally, managerialism alienates employees from one another, as well as from their managers. If employees compete against one another for limited rewards, then the spirit of camaraderie amongst them is battered. Consequently, it appears that the value of communalism works in different directions concerning how to organize a workplace.

On the other hand, an organization has the moral reason to commune with consumers and with shareholders, which probably provides reasons for it to steer employees towards the efficient production of goods and to deliver services efficiently. Therefore, a leader may use the managerialism approach to orientate the workplace if it fosters efficiency and makes the lives of its consumers and shareholders objectively better off.

The Afrocentric approach sees employees as important stakeholders in an organization. Typically, the relationship between them and their organization is intimate, meaning that the organization will not sacrifice its needs for the sake of the interests of consumers or other stakeholders. Even so, there are still some clear benefits of managerialism, especially in terms of meeting the demands of its customers and making money.

Here are examples of how a leader inspired by Afrocentric values may proceed with administration:

The leader may retain the use of a year-end bonus system to motivate workers but not strictly allocate it in proportion to workers' quantified output. Instead, the management award the same bonus to everybody who has done well or share profits in a more robust sense with them.

Again, the manager may use numerical targets that employees must meet, but he must never unilaterally set these targets. Instead, employees' unanimous agreement could be obtained first upon a discussion of what would be best for the organization and the employees.

Whom Should an Organization Aid?

An organization, public or private, cannot meet everybody's needs: rather, it should focus on the needs of its stakeholders. The question here is who is a stakeholder - a person for whom an organization has the moral reason to help?

In the Western orientation, there are two major reasons for helping people - they are people we have assumed a responsibility to help, or they are amongst the worst off and so owed help because of a general duty to assist. By this Rawlsian and Kantian approach, the manager/leader of an organization must take positive steps to carry out what it is contracted to do and to donate to those believed to be worse off in the organization's corporate social responsibility (CSR) programmes.

Apart from these two moral reasons for helping others, Afrocentrism espouses a third reason: collaborative relationship. If one has been in a collaborative relationship with others, one would have a strong moral reason to help these intimates instead of strangers, even if the strangers are worse off.

For example, one may decide to help one's children even if they are not doing badly, nor have they been promised any form of help. Only a few of us will voluntarily agree to help other people's children instead of helping our children or friends. Even if we did make such a promise to outsiders, we would still be obligated to help our children no matter what. The natural explanation of the obligation to help one's children or friends is that one has a lot in common with them over a long period. In a similar vein, one has the duty of helping one's neighbours and even co-workers regardless of how intense or cordial their relationship may be.

Applied to a business or entrepreneurial context, the Afrocentric principle of communalism presupposes that an organization would not only help those it has promised to help or those desperately in need of help, but also those with whom it shares some commonalities in values and culture. Again, an organization ought to identify with the community in which it operates because it is morally obligated to solidarize with such a community.

Another implication of this approach is that if an organization has a long-standing relationship with a particular client, the company's managers are morally bound to continue doing business with such a loyal and trusted client, even if a new client who is less costly knocks at the door. Though merely acknowledged, there is usually some moral cost to dumping a trusted client for another. In cases where there is no moral cost for dumping such a client or stakeholder, a possible explanation would be that the client failed to live up to their obligation to commune and has rather become exploitative.

Indigenous African Learning

Indigenous learning systems in African cultures aim at transmitting accumulated knowledge and wisdom to the young ones as a way of equipping them with the requisite behavioural competencies to take up leadership roles in the future and to ensure their community's continuity. The young learn how to farm, hunt, adapt to their environment in different seasons, prepare food, and run a home. They were taught the language, mores, norms, and the culture of their people. The learning methods applied were informal and practical, with the youths learning by participating in activities alongside their elders and by listening, watching, and doing.

Above all, they learned that behaviour and character mattered a lot to their community to whom behaviour or character would either bring honour or dishonour. This was ultimately training in citizenship and leadership. The most significant concern was hinged on the sort of life the young ones would live as community members and when they take up leadership positions in the community.

The more significant percentage of the cultures of sub-Saharan Africa emphasized social sensitivity, which made individuals subject themselves to the dictates of the group where the kinsfolk lived as members of one another's family. It was the goal of indigenous education to inculcate this sense of belongingness in the young ones. Indigenous learning sought to produce community members who were not selfish but pursued group interests; and fulfilled social obligations approved by tradition. Indigenous learning also drew on the spiritual dimension, which pervaded African life. Also, the African educational system encompassed the people's belief, which taught about the divine and the worship of God, nature, and the metaphysical world.

The practical approach to education in African culture emphasized the importance of experiential learning and experience to deal with lives' challenges. They believed that "a bird that has flown over a sea cannot be afraid of a river." The learning system utilized various methods, including work and play and religious rites, through songs, dances, proverbs, folklores, and customary services, transmitted or received within kinship ties.

In contrast, Western education emphasizes skills (cognitive domain) but not values (affective domain). The teaching relating to the cognitive domain is based on Western experience and is of little relevance to the African context.

Reconciliation through Justice: The case of Rwanda

Rwanda: A Brief Background

Rwanda is a landlocked country in the Great Rift Valley where the African Great Lakes region and East Africa converge. The country has a population of about 12.6 million living on 26,338 square km of land, making it the most densely populated country on the African mainland. Located a few degrees south of the Equator, Rwanda is bordered by Uganda, Tanzania, Burundi, and Congo DR. It must be noted that the country is multi-ethnic with Hutu (85%), Tutsi (14%, Twa (1%). It has a long history of mutual distrust between the two predominant tribes - the Hutus and Tutsis.

Christianity is the largest religion in the country, and the principal language is Kinyarwanda, spoken by most Rwandans, with English and French serving as additional official languages. Rwanda operates a presidential system of government in which President Paul Kagame of the Rwandan Patriotic Front (RPF) has been on the saddle since 2000.

Like other African countries, Rwanda has a colonial history, first under the Germans, and later Belgium, after the former was defeated in WWI. Like many other sub-Saharan countries, the "divide and rule" policy of the colonial masters left a poisoned political system in Rwanda by which the minority ruled over the majority, setting the stage for future conflicts.

However, scholars disagree on the origins of the differences between the Hutus and Tutsis; some believe the differences are derived from erstwhile social castes within a single person, while others believe the Hutu and Tutsi arrived in the country separately and from different locations.

Nonetheless, we know that the two former colonial masters perpetuated a pro-Tutsi policy of minority rule to the detriment of other ethnic groups, especially the majority Hutus. The Hutu population revolted in 1959 resulting in the massacre of numerous Tutsis, which eventually established an independent Hutu-dominated republic in 1962.

A 1973 military coup saw a change of leadership, but the pro-Hutu policy remained. The Tutsi-led Rwandan Patriotic Front later launched a civil war in 1990. The presidents of Burundi and Rwanda, both Hutus, were killed when their aircraft was shot down on 6 April 1994. The ensuing social tensions resulted in the 1994 genocide in which Hutu extremists killed an estimated 500,000 - 1,000,000 Tutsis and moderate Hutus. The RPF ended the genocide with a military victory.

How Were Leaders of Rwanda Able to Reconcile the Warring Factions?

The answers to this and other relevant questions are found in the intermarriage between indigenous African conflict resolution mechanisms with the orthodox justice system. Let's now examine some of the measures taken by Rwandan leaders to promote justice and douse tension in the aftermath of the genocide. While these do not suggest the absence of inter-group differences in a post-conflict setting of the absolute denial of Western leadership practices, they help highlight socio-political transformations that are possible if African leaders consciously embrace elements of Afrocentric leadership and governance principles.

Political Reforms in Rwanda

Post-conflict political reforms are critical to restoring confidence, integrity, reconciliation, and stability. Reform creates the opportunity for new roles and responsibilities to emerge and remove various aspects of the initial political order. Political reforms in Rwanda emphasized the transformation of systems and structures to expand political inclusion, primarily through political party activity and decentralization of power through local governments to communities. According to recent surveys carried out among Rwandans, the majority of participants believed that they took part in decisions that affected them through established and collectively accepted political processes.

Decentralization of governance (decision-making, fiscal and financial planning) to provincial and local levels resulted in significant political reforms in Rwanda. Surprisingly, these reforms contained elements of both Afrocentric and Western governance principles of conflict resolution. Rwandan local communities have now been empowered to serve as vehicles of transformation rather than becoming mere onlookers in the national project.

In 2001, Rwanda held the first local government elections under the new policy to decentralize governance. Among those elected nationally were 2,765 local council representatives, 106 town and district mayors, and an additional 424 new town district executives. The real achievement of this electoral reform was that new leadership was identified at all levels of society and elected. Subsequently, local governments begin to undertake development tasks hitherto handled by the central government in Kigali (the capital city), including access to education, rehabilitation of rural roads, provision of health facilities, poverty alleviation, dispute resolution, and other socio-political programmes.

Kagame's resoluteness, given the need to rid the country of conditions that occasioned genocide, has been the most visible in reforms to expand the space for political participation while guarding against any recourse to pre-genocidal and genocidal practices. Unlike the Western-based majoritarian 'winner-takes-all' approach to politics and governance, Rwanda's politics now runs on a consensus basis, with all parties represented in government, and according to the 2003 Rwanda Constitution, even the party with a majority of deputies cannot hold more than 50% of cabinet posts. Fluid as it may seem, such increased inclusiveness and participation in decision-making processes, and implementation of programmes in which communities have specific roles, reminisce of precolonial indigenous cultural practices and are central to stability in conflict-prone African societies.

Reconciliation through Justice

As mentioned earlier, indigenous African leadership ethos sees reconciliation as the main goal of a justice system. Similarly, the Rwandan national government tapped into local traditions through Gacaca and Ingando to achieve reconciliation and justice.

Other countries that have gone through devastating sectarian wars, for example, Liberia and the former Yugoslavia, often singled out perpetrators of heinous crimes and violence on the assumption that justice is best served by apprehending and prosecuting them.

In contrast, Rwanda achieved transformation and reduced tensions with a pragmatic approach that combines the typical retributive justice system favoured internationally to establish a National Unity and Reconciliation Commission (NURC) and a moderated traditional practice at the communal/national level through the Gacaca and Ingando systems. Despite these mechanisms' unevenness, many communities experienced a measure of justice and true reconciliation without undermining mainstream approaches to justice and without jeopardizing the need for peaceful coexistence.

Gacaca: Reconciliation and Justice in The African Way

Endogenous mechanisms of justice, rooted in African communal traditions, gained prominence in responding to local conflicts because they have evolved for extended periods and were adopted after consultations rather than being imposed or imported into Rwanda. The government's decision to formalize, moderate, and improve Gacaca highlights its relevance as a significant component of justice and reconciliation processes across local communities in Rwanda.

'Gacaca' is a traditional community-based approach to dispute resolution conducted by African elders in predominantly informal settings on issues involving land, marriage, property, and theft. The practice has been in place in major parts of the country since pre-colonial days. In 2002, the Kagame regime adopted Gacaca to try lesser crimes of genocide as an additional layer to provide justice and involve local communities in the reconciliation process. It operated alongside the national judicial system and the International Criminal Tribunal for Rwanda (ICTR).

The main feature of the system revolved around traditional weekly meetings. These served as local courts and have been used to adjudicate many cases related to genocide at the local level. Community members met weekly to consider issues and other disputes in the community collectively and to give evidence and testimony that would aid the elected judges to give their judgement on the matter.

Intended to provide relief to an overwhelmed justice sector with thousands of the accused who could potentially face trial, Gacaca became a visionary approach to draw grassroots communities into the work of the NURC, as well as complement other national efforts aimed at addressing the legacies of genocide. To date, the Gacaca system has continued to celebrate its contribution towards achieving lasting peace in Rwanda. A Social Cohesion survey of the NURC in 2008 found that 96% of survivors and 83% of prisoners believed that the Gacaca system was a better way of handling their cases and eradicating impunity in the country than traditional courts.

Ingando: African Reflective Practice

Ingando is a traditional Rwandan practice of demobilizing regular activities to reflect and find solutions to communal challenges and the

Table 14: Differences between Africans and Western people in conflict resolution. Source: Adapted from Blunt and Jones (1997)

Westerners	Africans
Win/lose tactics within clearly defined structures, and procedures are applied when managing conflict.	Within a framework of morals, the immediate family, supervisors, and elders manage conflict.
Members enter into negotiation to control the outcome.	Members enter into a dialogue towards an outcome.
The outcome is in terms of rightness or wrongness.	The outcome is in terms of fairness or unfairness.
Inherent in this system is violence and disharmony according to sets of rules and standards.	Inherent in this system is a search for reconciliation and harmony.

re-integration of convicts into societies through special programmes. In pre-modern times, traditional rulers and local chiefs often mobilized their people to come together and reflect on dire situations like wars, disease outbreaks, droughts, and also to find collective solutions. This is a form of the African communal system of creating a level playing field for political participation.

With support from the Rwandan national government, the NURC revived Ingando to engage convicts and communities in reconciliatory dialogue. As a complement to Gacaca, the main objective of Ingando is to transform relationships from conflict into peaceful coexistence at individual and communal levels.

Ingando involves face-to-face meetings where national issues are discussed and themes covered include: a history of Rwanda, analysis of Rwanda's problems, discussions of socioeconomic problems, human rights, duties, obligations, and leadership. Prisoners needed to participate in these programmes to reflect on their crimes and commit themselves to peace before they were released back into society.

Nowadays, the programme takes the form of civic education. It has been extended nationwide to include: students, traders, women, youths, leaders (both public and private), and erstwhile perpetrators of genocide. About 3,000 students attend Ingando retreats yearly at the National Ingando Centre in Ruhengeri. The NURC, working through local councils, schools, and other community structures, provides logistics and other forms of support.

Conclusion

This chapter has laid bare the concept of Afrocentric leadership based on African values of "MAAT," which can serve as an excellent alternative to the largely ineffectual Western paradigm in the African context. The reader is probably surprised that Africa possesses such a clear leadership philosophy that can be applied equally in public and private settings to promote leadership performance and effectiveness. The character traits or behavioural competencies expected of an effective leader in Africa have also been highlighted, and they are simple enough to be codified into learning modules to be taught in leadership development institutions across the landscape of sub-Saharan Africa.

Evidence to support the applicability of some of these principles was eventually provided in resolving the Rwanda Genocide Crisis of the 1990s, which nearly broke up the country into pieces. The Rwandans resorted to the African way of justice administration, which paved the way for genuine reconciliation and forgiveness in contrast to what is obtainable elsewhere with a similar crisis. Therefore, we safely conclude that indigenous African leadership principles are practicable and applicable to solving the numerous challenges confronting the region if only African leaders are bold enough to embrace, research, fine-tune, and utilize the Afrocentric perspectives enunciated in this chapter

8

SUB-SAHARAN AFRICA: THE WAY FORWARD

Chapter 8

A united and developed Africa wedded to the basic values of the respect for life that constitutes the undercurrent of its traditional civilizations will impress humanity with the joy and significance of life. An Africa united and prosperous; an Africa united and powerful will be a balancing factor in a world of solidarity, dialogue, and peace

- Edem Kodjo.

Leadership is one of the most critical elements for measuring and ensuring organizational effectiveness. With a history of bad governance, slave trade, colonialism, low productivity, low workforce morale, and a social disconnect between leaders and the masses, the development of SSA into a region of political stability and economic prosperity calls for extraordinary leadership equipped with relevant leadership concepts and skills. Good leaders can go beyond the reactive, quick fix, immediate gratification, and traditional approaches, which are required for long-term socio-economic survival. With a firm commitment to enable, empower and liberate Africans, only these leaders will ensure the region's competitive advantage for the future.

This final chapter urges Africa to look inwards, find what works for us, and adopt it unapologetically. The chapter recognizes that we are different peoples with varied ways of life, as well as a multiplicity of cultures, traditions, norms, mores, and values. We must resist the culture of placing square pegs in round holes - using Western leadership structures to lead Africans. In the end, attempts shall be made to recommend workable solutions calling on Africans to take decisive actions rather than going round in circles in perpetuity.

The Need for sub-Saharan Africa to Look Inwards

One of the factors frequently omitted from studies of leadership in Africa is a consideration of the potential significance of the cultural context within which leadership and management are practised. Recent studies have shown increasing awareness of this important factor. The discussions in this book have reinforced the importance of this line of research for better insight into current leadership failures on the continent and to generate guidelines for effective leadership development interventions.

The conceptual framework presented in this book is the first step in providing a coherent model for future research. It sees macro cultures of African societies as informing the expectations, goals, relationships, and resources allocation decisions of African leaders. These, in turn, shape their decisions and behavioural patterns within organizations and their overall contributions to organizational performance. The framework helps throw more light on the nature of leadership in Africa and the potentials for paradigm shifts that can improve governance, organizational performance, and economic development on the continent.

The awareness that all cultures are constantly subjected to pressure for change from both internal and external factors provides African leaders with opportunities to facilitate cultural change processes in the organizations that they lead. Thus, the book's key message is that leadership development agents in Africa must exhibit attentiveness grounded in existing cultural values. It is argued that not all aspects of African culture act as constraints to effective leadership. Comprehensive empirical investigations into the impact of dominant African cultural attributes on leadership and organizational performance are urgently required to guide leadership development initiatives in the continent.

Encouraging informed debate on the success or otherwise of Western leadership and management ideas in developing countries is desirable. The discussion must be genuinely multilateral, and it should welcome differences of opinion. This book argues that such debate has tended to and tends to be one-sided and too culturally biased. For example, it has been argued that the notion of sustainable human development as espoused by the United Nations Development Programme (UNDP) gives prominence to an ideological precept - popular participation in political and organizational decision-making - central to Western democratic tradition. Similar preoccupations are evident in Western notions of leadership.

So far, this book's brief discussion of leadership has revealed that Western ideas have failed to lift SSA out of poverty. It can be further argued that these concepts and theories are not widely applicable to the region, given the major differences in values concerning authority, group loyalties, and interpersonal harmony. Leadership in the West is a follower and performance-oriented, and therefore inclined to be more participatory. Concerns for employee welfare mask an overriding interest in the performance of the individual and the organization. In contrast, SSA leadership orientation is known for maintaining communal harmony, which has deep cultural roots that can override short-term commercial considerations but still be in the organization's long-term interests. Also, the performance of economies and organizations is a function of much more than patterns of leadership alone, contrary to mainstream opinion.

Conclusion

This research on the sub-Saharan African leadership phenomenon has revealed a wide range of issues and concepts about leadership in the region that warrant further exploration and elaboration. Sadly, there is insufficient space for me to explore all of these issues in this book. However, many substantial points do stand out.

Firstly, it has become evident that this form of research (that is, narrative research) in this kind of setting (that is, SSA) has important things to reveal about the nature of leadership. This research, and the data collected therein, indicate that SSA has its unique leadership styles dating back to the precolonial era. Contrary to some Western notions, sub-Saharan African societies established precolonial empires and kingdoms. They also experimented with different political systems with features as advanced as those found in that era's Western societies. The common elements of these indigenous cultures are the concepts of communalism and collective responsibility. Surprisingly, these sophisticated practices can still be observed in some contemporary SSA societies, notwithstanding the incursion of Arab and Western ideas into the region.

The second set of issues and implications surround the context of leadership in SSA. European incursion and the subsequent colonial rule negatively impacted leadership institutions and social cohesion in the region. After the Berlin Conference of 1885, for example, Africans of the same ethnic group suddenly found themselves separated between different colonial territories. Those of different ethnic affiliations were lumped together in artificially created nation-states. More so, the so-called 'mission to civilize Africa' did not make the continent a better place to live for the inhabitants, despite the millions of African lives sacrificed in the despicable experiment.

While it is easy to argue in support of the shift towards "global" styles of leadership and management (typically Western in origin) and tempting to dismiss more "traditional" practices, neither is advisable. The exploration of Western leadership concepts through colonialism and neocolonialism in SSA has revealed that it is beneficial and destructive at the time. The same also applies to mainstream Western management practices adopted by many international organizations and multinationals operating in Africa.

As such, Obiakor (2004) argues that African leadership is 'still tied to European-centred frameworks,' a situation he insists is 'counter-productive to the sacred existence of African people. He concludes that leadership as a concept in African institutions should rather be 'tied to the apron strings of African cultural values and that Africans must shift their paradigms to produce effective leadership across the continent.

The third set of issues surrounds the application of leadership. This research on SSA has shown that leadership begins with accepting and taking up one's role within a community (or social) setting. By viewing the concept of "self in the community" as the essential building block of shared or distributed leadership, we can personalize and apply these concepts to modern African societies, thus moving beyond abstract and diffuse representation to an appreciation of how humans interact within the social milieu. This does not signify a return to psychological theories of leadership but an acknowledgement of the importance of recognizing one's position within a social system and the opportunities that this affords for taking up a leadership role. Such an idea is rooted in the MAAT or Ubuntu's concept within an African context, as discussed earlier. In this context, a person is because others are, and this poses a powerful challenge to Western philosophy, as does the Chinese philosophy of Yin and Yang duality.

It is virtually impossible to determine what makes someone a good leader, particularly in the light of conflicting value systems around the world. This book has expounded a conception of culture-centred leadership that is under-appreciated or unappreciated in the West. Specifically, it has discussed the traditional African principles of leadership based on prizing people by their capacity to relate communally. It also seeks to argue that these prescriptions constitute plausible alternatives to Western leadership principles applied willy-nilly in SSA.

Supposing the attempt to ground various dimensions of leadership on an Afrocentric perspective has been prima facie attractive; other matters also merit investigation. For example, we may need to know if communion is compatible with entrepreneurship and innovation, which are important for businesses and organizations with a significant influence on the public? Or, are these best justified by individualist and predominantly Western values? Is there a characteristically indigenous African approach to time and, if so, is it a function of communalism? Is it compatible enough with organizational efficiency?

If this book has been revealing and thought-provoking enough, the reader will agree that these important questions merit answers in future research.

In conclusion, as we proceed more into the 21st Century and seriously address issues of leadership failure in SSA. It is essential that we not only take into account but also celebrate our different legacies, heritage, and indigenous cultures, to appreciate better and understand the multitude of ways in which issues of leadership can be understood and expressed. This will benefit Africans, including leaders, politicians, students, managers, employees, and even expatriates working in SSA, and help expand and refresh their African worldview by offering new insights into the phenomenon of leadership and its pivotal role in the social management of societies and nation

Recommendations

The crisis of leadership and governance in SSA results in continued poverty for millions of African masses, under-development, and deepened dependence on Western ideas. The causes of this crisis have been identified. But high among them is that many African countries lack a broadly shared vision of the future that effectively meets the demands of globalization with local values.

To overcome the perennial leadership challenges, a Zimbabwean official of the World Bank once noted that African leaders must:

(i)   Identify and address their strengths and weaknesses

(ii)   Understand the challenges they face as participants in a rapidly changing world

(iii)   Share and refine their respective visions of the society they would like to live in; and

(iv)   Lead by example in building this society.

Along the same lines, other scholars have argued that Sub-Saharan Africa stands on the verge of great opportunity, which must be grasped. African leaders increasingly understand the reasons to redefine where they want to take the region and look inwards to find solutions to the challenges confronting their people. This has been articulated by various African policymakers (both public and private). The challenge now is to take this forward forcefully.

The new initiative is being accompanied by a growing consensus among African scholars that Africans themselves should lead the development agenda. The reorientation of leadership concepts should be at the centre of development efforts. Sub-Saharan Africa is the only region of the world where poverty is rising rather than abating. Decisive action is needed if we want to cut severe poverty by half in the next few decades. We need more growth, at least 5% to 10%, and we need to ensure enough effective leaders to lead the way.

From an Afrocentric perspective, recommendations for solutions to African developmental challenges must emanate from Africans' concerns, interests, and viewpoints, based on their understanding of the challenges.

Speaking in concrete terms, what are the imperatives required to reposition SSA for development within the global system?

Redefining leadership in Africa

So far, this book has shown how and why Western leadership principles have failed in Africa. It has also highlighted reasons why indigenous African leadership concepts will serve it better as the foundation for its development initiatives.

To move forward with these Afrocentric ideas, SSA will need to set an agenda, goals, and targets that are well informed by a sound knowledge base and a vision that is vigorously pursued, not mere dreams that die with the dreamer. Indeed, through the strengthening of democracy, civil society becomes a tool to enhance sustainable peace, security, stability, and development, and there can be no civil society without the people's collective and direct involvement.

Much international spotlight has been focused on the severity of SSA's challenges. Addressing those challenges in a new cooperative spirit should nurture and sustain change and renewal in the region. But challenges cannot be tackled with inappropriate solutions. Urging the citizens to get involved in all spheres of leadership involves redefining leadership in SSA to develop a new breed of leaders who commit to making personal sacrifices in the public interest.

Building consensus

What can African leaders and people do to resolve the developmental challenges confronting them?

An answer to this question in the Afrocentric perspective is reconciliation, which will be the basis for the following public policy recommendations. Reconciliation is an important method for managing and resolving conflicts and other shared governance, organizational, economic development, and participation activities. Building consensus and collaborating reflect a deep concern for the interests of the people in dispute.

This conflict resolution approach emphasizes problem-solving and pursues an outcome that gives both parties what they want. The collaboration framework is often regarded as the best approach to conflict resolution because it helps to satisfy both parties with a goal of "I win" and "you win."

Judicial reforms

The judicial system of the countries of sub-Saharan Africa must not relent in taking steps to install an effective administration of the justice system. As such, there is an urgent need to restructure the judiciary system in most of those countries. It could be argued that institutional reforms can also lead to the transformation of the judicial system. It is also likely to positively impact other areas, such as combating corruption and all forms of financial malpractices.

However, the bone of contention is the fair and impartial administration of justice where nobody is above the law or constitutional provisions of any country in SSA. The judicial system also needs to keep abreast of the growing best practice in the field. The involvement of indigenous legal practitioners through the judicial system in conflict resolution should be regarded as part of the sustainable development process. This is necessary to curtail apathy towards conflict resolution among legal practitioners. The restructuring of legal education to cover a complete course of study in alternative dispute resolution (ADR) mechanisms based on African cultural values is already in practice in some African countries like Ghana, Nigeria, and Rwanda. These have significantly contributed to maintaining the peace in those places.

Ensuring accountability

Employees are more engaged when their managers effectively hold them or their teams accountable for results. An individual employee may be doing great work, but others on the team may be lagging. If a manager or leader does not checkmate this situation, it may discourage other team members from exerting themselves. Leaders should be clear about expectations and be sure that employees clearly understand and accepts these expectations. They need to be consistent in delivering rewards for meeting and exceeding expectations or for not meeting them.

With leaders adopting the right attitude and demonstrating good intentions through appropriate perceivable behaviour, it would be only a matter of time before employees further down the hierarchy start reflecting the attitudes and values of the leadership.

The final step is where employees, through empowerment and inclusion, begin to assume responsibility and build meaningful relationships with other employees and their leaders. In this way, employees can give back to the organization, as well as creating a virtuous flow of energy and ideas for the overall benefit of the organization.

Although this process may sound simplistic, the beauty lies in its simplicity. What is needed is a change of heart and a genuine concern for others on the part of African leaders and business managers.

The main obstacles to the process will be individuals who do not want to change their attitude and those who do not care for or about others.

But leaders who cannot discipline or change themselves should not expect to change others. And those who do not care for their followers should not expect followers to respect them automatically. Humility is a virtue that African leaders should embrace at all levels of the leadership spectrum.

Identifying leadership potential

When identifying leadership potential to develop responsible leadership for SSA development, it is important to first look at the big picture. African countries and organizations need to ensure an alignment of the priorities, objectives, and strategic focus from the regional level down to the national and departmental levels and to ensure that they all have a shared vision and a sense of purpose. From there, Africans can establish connections between these institutions at the implementation stage. Using higher education institutions as the foundation, African governments can ensure that well-trained graduates with appropriate leadership skills are produced who will shoulder the responsibility of transforming their countries in the nearest future.

The focus should be on ensuring SSA's competitiveness, economic integration, development, and sustainability at the regional level. To achieve these feats, the region should aim to improve the standard of formal education (critical for achieving competitiveness in the 21st Century) and ensure that it also focuses on creating decent and sustainable livelihoods, making possible the attainment of economic development and sustainability. Accordingly, at the educational level, the role of institutions is to show commitment to research and innovation in learning.

Recognition

It is important for leaders to consistently and frequently recognize their employees or followers for doing excellent work. This can be a simple "thank you" or "congratulations" message or allocating organizational awards and bonuses to deserving employees. Recognition often has a way of impacting positively on employee engagement.

Enhancing Good Governance

Good governance is also about accountability and depends on information, transparency, and resourcefulness. Because the difficulty in ensuring inclusiveness and accountability in governance is complex, many approaches have evolved to expand and defend inclusiveness and hold governments and government officials more accountable.

For policymakers striving to improve their economy's regulatory environment for business, a good place to start is to find out how it compares with the regulatory environment in other economies. Nation capacity building is a long-term process. It needs long-term strategies and policies whose impact will prevent the emergence of conditions that gave rise to stagnated economic growth.

Leadership Training and Culture

This is the belief that becoming a good leader is possible when training grounds are available and properly positioned for great acculturation for the youth. Therefore, SSA needs to formulate new training methods for future leadership positions based on Afrocentric concepts.

This is not to say that Africans should reject Western leadership and management training methods. But rather fresh ideas should be introduced, which will incorporate African cultural peculiarities and experiences. If anything, this training will develop leaders who have their peoples' interests in mind and are competent enough to handle the complex problems besetting their countries. The phrase "placing square pegs in square holes" comes to mind in this context.

The Emergence of New Role Models

Africa's 21st Century will be secure if there are enough role models for leadership 'apprentices' or 'students' to emulate or to inspire them. In the contemporary private sector, examples of such leaders include Mo Ibrahim, Elon Musk, Jim Ovia, Ngozi Okonjo-Iweala, Omawumi Evelyn Urhobo, Susana Edjang, Ifrah Ahmed, Lucy Quist, and others. In the public sector, there are names like Nelson Mandela, Thabo Mbeki, Paul Kagame, Goodluck Jonathan, and John Kuffour. However, SSA still needs more of these exemplary leaders who have distinguished themselves in their chosen endeavours. After all, the youths learn faster by example and not by experience or empty rhetoric.

Reforming Public Institutions

Public institutions are central to good governance because they are the vehicles through which government provides services to the citizens. Democratic reforms and efforts to institutionalize good governance will achieve little to nothing unless the bureaucratic public institutions that anneal good governance are reformed. Indeed, good governance remains a mirage in SSA, and this cannot be delinked from the misconduct of her leaders and ineffective public institutions that are, more or less, relics of colonial rule.

Moreover, African governments cannot conform to the imperatives of good governance unless institutions through which they serve the citizens function effectively and efficiently. Governments, at all levels, must reform fraying and dysfunctional public institutions that prevent citizens from deriving optimal benefits from their governance system. Stressing the need to reform public institutions in Nigeria, former Governor of Nigeria's Central Bank, Professor Charles Soludo, noted that "to make rapid progress, the institutions of the state need restructuring and strengthening. The focus is to eliminate perverse institutions, rebuild or create institutions that are developmental in orientation, tie the hands of government from arbitrary behaviour and circumscribe it to behave in a manner that is socially optimal."

In essence, public institutions in SSA require vast structural and attitudinal adjustments that will curtail corruption and inefficiency and expand the frontiers of accountability and transparency. Public agencies should no longer be allowed to function in an atmosphere of corruption and executive interference.

Competence, efficiency, autonomy, and transparency should become the watchword of African public institutions. For this to happen, there should be no alternatives to recruiting competent and honest employees or civil servants who have the autonomy and integrity to act in the best interest of the public. Also, efforts must be made to encourage citizens and government officials to treat public institutions with a different mindset, emphasizing accountability, honesty, patriotism, and transparency over the pursuit of selfish interests.

Ultimately, SSA will be much better to live if leaders pursue self-restraint and subordinate their selfish interests to the overriding interests of their nations. Good governance may not necessarily address all of SSA's problems, but most of the problems may prove amenable to a solution once effective leadership is in place.

Improving Governance and Resolving Conflicts

It can be seen that well-managed countries with effective leadership institutions and sound policies tend to be more prosperous than poorly managed countries. Over the last few decades, dysfunctional leadership and bad governance have taken a heavy toll on SSA's development. Skewed budget allocations, endemic corruption, and a corroded fabric of leader-follower relations often continue to undermine the potential for successful development and even foster conflict in some cases.

Therefore, countries of sub-Saharan Africa need urgent improvement in governance if they are to surmount the developmental challenges confronting them. They also need to build on the few success stories, scale them up, and replicate them across the region.

Increasing Competitiveness

Despite globalization, many SSA countries are at the risk of being marginalized. Over the last decade, Africa has fallen behind in terms of both investments and productivity. In some countries, efforts have been made to improve the investment climate - but much remains to be done. And the small size of most SSA economies is also a hindrance: the median African country has a GDP of $2-$3 billion and a population of 15 million. These are small markets compared with markets in other regions of the world like Western Europe, Latin America, South East Asia, and the Middle East. For most African countries, the challenge is to create a more significant economic space with more opportunities for investors and entrepreneurs.

As suggested earlier, regional cooperation and integration are part of the solution. Diversification of the economies is another way of promoting economic development in SSA. Better infrastructure is also important. Or how could businesses operate with phone systems that do not work, frequent power outages, and poorly maintained roads? And how can SSA compete effectively in today's global market when only about 0.1 per cent of internet content is generated from there, despite having about 16.7 per cent of the world's population? It is estimated that SSA's loss of world trade has cost it not less than $50 billion annually since the late 1960s - we can only imagine what that money could do.

Restoring a Cultural Sense of Value

This book has shown that colonial influence and Western imperialism have succeeded in eroding many cultural values which SSA used to be known for. Value can be defined as those behaviours that are acceptable in society, and it is synonymous with morality. Cultural values determine how individuals will behave in a community, as well as when participating in politics. Unlike Western cultures, African cultural values are rooted in communalism and humanness. Broadly speaking, communalism promotes public access to societal resources so that every member has a share in the benefits of such resources.

There is no gainsaying that these cultural values of communalism and humanness are gradually overridden by the Western culture of individualism and materialism, which encourages greed and selfish behaviours among Africans.

Many Western scholars particularly consider African culture a barrier to development. Consequently, at the introduction of formal or colonial education in SSA, school curricula were fashioned to make students unconsciously assimilate Western values, languages, and ideologies and to see indigenous cultural values as inferior. Many schools in the region are proud to use one Western education curriculum or the other, while indigenous African knowledge is frowned at and ignominiously dismissed. Indeed, education became a tool in the imperialists' hands to superimpose their foreign ideas of learning and behaviour on unwary Africans, without room for Afrocentric and culture-based learning methods.

Since education was used to put down Africans, education can also be used as a tool of cultural revitalization and moral education in Africa. This requires the decolonization of Africa's educational system by incorporating curricula that re-teach students to understand and appreciate cultural values of honesty, hard work, contentment, humility, patriotism, and appreciation of indigenous culture, knowledge, food, clothes, and other positive aspects of African culture.

Implementation of African-centred Policies That Seek Only the Interest of Africans

There is a need to prioritize citizens' needs and interests in policy formulation and implementation. This book has shown how the main development strategies adopted by many SSA countries have been rooted in the Western development experience. These policies sometimes seek to protect foreign interests to the detriment of the African masses. One prominent feature of mainstream development theories such as globalization, Millennium Development Goals (MDGs), modernization, good governance, and SAP is trade liberalization. With the poor state of SSA's infrastructure and limited productive capacity to compete at the international level, trade liberalization only makes African economies dumping ground for Western products and inadvertently killing the region's infant industries and worsening poverty.

Meanwhile, even though the IMF and the World Bank insist that African countries open up their economies, Western countries, based on WTO agreements, have strategic means of instituting trade restrictions, which prevent African countries from accessing their markets.

While the IMF and other IFIs positioned themselves as Africa's development partners, it is important to note that these institutions also represent the West and often ensures that local socioeconomic conditions are made conducive for Western "exploitation." For example, in Nigeria's oil industry, the IFIs cannot be forgiven for how the oil revenue has bred corruption and increased environmental degradation and poverty in the oil-rich Niger Delta area. It has been reported by Amnesty International, UK that "Shell BP is complicit in the terror campaign carried out by various Nigerian governments against Ogoni communities protesting against oil spills and environmental pollution in the 1990s".

Besides, some IFIs, especially the Export Credit Agencies (ECAs) operated by the governments of most industrialized countries, finance oil projects without demanding that the projects meet minimum developmental, environmental, or social standards. This explains the decrepit levels of environmental pollution and degradation of the communities in the Niger Delta oil-producing region of Nigeria.

For this and many reasons, this book argues that nobody can protect African interests better than Africans themselves. No international development policy can take care of Africa's needs and interests better than a leadership pursuing citizen-centred and home-grown policies.

Leadership Pipeline and Creativity

It is also important for African leaders to design systems that facilitate learning from the multiple sources of leadership and management ideas and integrate them into new and appropriate tools that would improve the quality of management deliverables at all levels of society. A weak learning process would mean that other resources within the continent would remain fragmented and their potential left untapped.

On the other hand, a robust learning process would uplift the citizens of Africa, which will, in turn, boost their capacities and creative potential. This will invariably help checkmate the current state of inaction and perpetual helplessness prevailing on the continent.

Moreover, scholars of organizational learning see employee empowerment as one of the criteria for knowledge development and creativity. In this context, the autocratic leadership styles that still dominate many African organizations have impinged on the development of a learning culture and knowledge acquisition.

The current understanding is that African employees exhibit a higher propensity to follow instructions than adopt a critical attitude or mindset to accomplishing assigned tasks. These observations corroborate comprehensive empirical investigations, which are already in the public domain. We need insights into how learning is encouraged in African organizations and the roles that leaders can play to facilitate the process.

Utilize and Export Leadership Excellence

Once SSA countries have learnt to develop and utilize their knowledge, they will also need to document and share it with others. Individual countries of the region must believe in themselves, and then be open to sharing their expertise with other African nations and the rest of the world. In this regard, agencies like Brand Africa can help propagate Afro-optimism. For example, South Africa hosted a successful 2010 FIFA World Cup and surprised the entire world with its organizational prowess and ability. The country is already leveraging organizational skills acquired from this and other experiences to improve industries across Africa. Imagine what sub-Saharan African economies would look like without South African brands like MTN, MultiChoice, Shoprite, Vodacom, and others?

Indeed, African organizations need to engage more in responsible strategic partnering across the continent and beyond as a fulcrum for expansion, remaining relevant, and conducting business ethically.

By following these steps, a new breed of leaders can be developed, and a framework provided for projecting into the future we desire.

Promoting Good Governance Through MAAT

MAAT Defined

Just like many African concepts, the concept of MAAT is not easily definable. It has been described as an African worldview and a determining factor in the formation of perceptions that affect socio-political realities in indigenous cultures. It has also been described as a philosophy of life representing humanity, personhood, morality, and values.

Indeed, there are common concepts of MAAT to be found in almost all African cultures in terms of beliefs, practices, and value systems. According to how it is identified in different African cultures, the most abiding principle of this African orientation is known as MAAT or Omoluwabism or Ubuntu. MAAT is a way of life that has sustained indigenous African societies for centuries.

MAAT is the art of being human, and people live out their MAAT values in the same way that Christians or Muslims strive to be good and to do good. Inter alia, its characteristics include humanness, which comprises values of universal brotherhood, respect for others, non-racial orientation, and environmental sustainability.

Therefore, MAAT may be defined as a deep-rooted, all-inclusive African worldview that pursues humanness, caring, sharing, and associated values that ensure qualitative community life in indigenous African societies.

Implications of MAAT on the Community and Work Ethics

MAAT has far-reaching implications for an individual's priorities in life, including their attitude and behaviour towards others. This means that other people, their joy or pain, are important to the person who beliefs in MAAT. To pardon or forgive is an essential aspect of the MAAT spirit. Therefore, MAAT implies the absence of class in its truest sense since everyone is the same and equal. MAAT's ethical values can be applied to different areas of life, such as:

- Business - through teamwork, sustainability, collective learning, a community focus, and as an alternative to exploitative capitalism;

- Politics - the African Renaissance;

- Corporate governance - through the values of fairness in justice, collective responsibility, and humility;

- Conflict resolution - through the ethos of truth commissions as witnessed in Rwanda and South Africa; and

- Restorative justice - through the use of dialogue and collective restitution

MAAT is a cultural framework to understand African life. It also has a striking resemblance to the tenets of the Social Interest Theory in Individual Psychology. The fundamental belief in MAAT is that "a person is a person through others." Thus, a person exists relative to the group he or she belongs to. This is often manifested in anti-individualistic behaviour toward the survival of the community if the person is to survive and serve the community. A person's responsibility is not concealed through community effort but participation in community work, which enhances or diminishes a person's self-recognition. In effect, a person is a person through what they do.

Workplaces that are grounded in MAAT orientation are likely to make workers more comfortable than those based on self-serving leadership styles.

Describing MAAT

MAAT is a call to service and participation. It is a call to serve humanity in practical ways. Its values connect, link, and bind people together in a community. It is an important principle where those who are strong help the weak. MAAT also deals with feelings of compassion and making life more comfortable for others. These acts help to instil sense into the life of others and even into one's life. The following descriptions of MAAT are given as recipes for leadership in any given context:

• A philosophy of tolerance

• A non-racial value system in which everyone is treated as a human being

• a philosophical orientation that accepts human family as one, despite different racial groups

• The dignity of human personality

• Supreme goodness that transforms people into living souls in the image of God

Practical examples of MAAT behaviour include:

• The way one greets others in a friendly manner;

• The way one talks in a positive manner;

• The way one walks in an unstressed way;

• The way one respectfully treats others; and

• The way one practices moral values by caring for others.

The Case for Effective Leadership in SSA

Effective leadership requires African leaders to steer away from self-indulgent attitudes and policies of the past and refocus on creative ways of providing solutions to the myriads of problems besetting their countries and embracing the new norms of good governance, which requires leaders to overhaul ingrained practices that shift their attention to the virtues of good governance.

Without attitudinal changes, the prospects of institutionalizing good governance will remain nothing but mere fantasy. A good and effective government is a government where leaders accept and internalize the norms and values of democracy, appreciate and understand the scope and limitations of their powers, and always act in full awareness and sensitivity to the democratic norms of accountability, transparency, and respect for the rule of law.

Effective leadership requires two essential, perhaps indispensable traits, which are humility and restraint. Leaders must be humble enough to serve their people, tending to their concerns and welfare. They should also exercise some restraint, know and respect the limits of their authority, and always act in full awareness of the extent of their powers and authority.

If Africa is to break with its grim status quo, it has to do something different. It is said that doing the same thing over and over again and expecting different results is madness. If SSA countries leverage their rich diversity in human and material resources, they must start doing things differently and innovatively. After all, no country has ever achieved high development goals through imitation or using resources that are not indigenous to it - not China, America, Germany, Switzerland, or Russia. Hence, this book advocates an

African leadership approach that is culture-based, accountable, ethical, relevant, and responsible if Africans are to galvanize their resources and create a better future for themselves – one where SSA operates as an equal competitive partner at the global stage. Also, this book recommends that further studies be conducted to explore the application of Afrocentric leadership ethos in individual countries and organizations in SSA as a way of attaining sustainable development.

This book suggests that the antidote to most SSA's problems is good leadership anchored on African values. This is because Africans have unique ways of solving their societal problems, partly or wholly abandoned due to the overbearing influence of Western imperialism. It is high time Africans dug up these forgotten leadership and management principles that are most suited to their peculiar culture and experiences.

Agenda for Future Research

Initiating change within African leadership and management culture requires additional knowledge that future research must seek to provide. Research work is needed in many areas of African leadership discourse. Two of such areas are listed here for immediate attention:

(1) Leadership development strategies

(2) Leadership and organizational performance.

Leadership Development Strategies

We need guidelines from researchers on what kind of leadership development strategies to adopt in SSA. The concept of hybridization and cross-cultural perspectives introduced by John Kuada and Terence Jackson must be studied in terms of organizational performance. The understanding of these scholars is that African leadership development must not depend exclusively on practices imported from the West but must be built on ideas and principles from non-Western cultures combined with selected African cultural values.

This perspective is consistent with the arguments of other scholars such as Richard Bolden and Philip Kirk that appropriate management constructs and models must be developed and couched with culturally relevant languages and concepts. These researchers' recent publications show us that the influence of different religious beliefs and associated practices combine with gender, age, and ethnic networks to shape emerging African leadership practices. They also noted some evidence of change and tension between past experiences and future aspirations for leadership, with a growing emphasis on the need to situate leadership practices in the communities and organizations in which the leaders are located. These emergent perspectives require more elaborate and cross-national empirical investigations.

Leadership and Organizational Performance

A great deal of the empirical literature on African leadership and management reviewed in this book is based on studies conducted about seven or more years ago. Qualitative leadership will help to halt Africa's economic woes and place it on a consistent path of growth and poverty alleviation. In that case, we need some more current knowledge to determine how the existing leadership practices influence the efficiency and effectiveness of decisions and activities in private and public sector organizations in SSA. For instance, we need to know whether African organizations are still characterized by centralized power structures, high degrees of uncertainty, and bureaucratic resistance to change.

We also need to know whether extended family orientations or the assertions that African leaders sacrifice organizational goals for their personal and family gains are still valid and still exert dominant influences on the leaders' behaviour and organizational performance.

The issue of what types of leadership styles improve organizational performance in Africa also deserves research attention. Would the Afrocentric leadership orientation exemplified by "MAAT" be the most suitable for African organizations, or would it be more effective in combination with Western leadership concepts? This question cries for further research.

Furthermore, this book has suggested that Ubuntu and good leadership, as well as governance principles, are compatible and complementary. Though some scholars consider Ubuntu as a local idea, yet most elements of Ubuntu are universal. It is the concept of humanness and shared values of the human race in general. Values such as dignity, empathy, respect, harmony, and cooperation between members of a society or organization are not exclusively African but involve the human race. However, it remains an ideal since it is not yet practised in the global village.

This book agrees that only a leader who has a value-based orientation of leadership and who could appreciate the existing value systems within a team or an organization can achieve role modelling.

Thus, when Ubuntu is appropriately implemented in SSA, it can help promote team effectiveness and eventually institutionalize organizational effectiveness and promote good governance.

In truth, there is an urgent need for African leadership practitioners to dig deeper into what is needed to reposition their countries and for a reawakening of their leadership capacity. Such introspection could be focused on the following probing questions:

- How do we incorporate the spiritual beliefs of participants?

- How do we balance leadership and followership?

- How can we support the long-term needs of leadership development? Is it by supporting young and second-tier leaders as compared to only supporting individuals or only individual organizations?

The discoveries that this type of self-analysis can reveal should be proactively shared with the outside world to benefit international organizations and African development partners.

Bibliography

6-D Model of National Culture. (n.d.). Hofstede's Cultural Dimensions for Selected Countries. Retrieved from https://geerthofstede.com/

Abegunrin, O. (2009). Africa in Global Politics in the Twenty-first Century: A Pan African Perspective. New York: Palgrave Macmillan.

Acemoglu, D., Robinson, J. A., & Woren, D. (2012). Why Nations Fail: The Origins of Power, Prosperity, and Poverty, Vol. 4. New York: Crown Business.

Achebe, C. (1983). The Trouble with Nigeria. Enugu: Fourth Dimension.

Adedeji, A. (1993). Africa within the World: Beyond Dispossession and Dependence. London: Zed Books.

Adedeji, A. (1999). Comprehending and Mastering African Conflicts. London: Zed Books.

Adejumobi, S. (2000). Elections in Africa: a fading shadow of democracy. International Political Science Review, 21(1): 68.

Adeleye, I. (2011). Theorizing Human Resource Management in Africa: Beyond Cultural Relativism. African Journal of Business

Management, 5(6): 2028-2039.

Adeoye, A. A. (2005). Multinational Corporations in South Africa: Armed Conflict and Majority Rule in Southern Africa. International Review of Politics and Development, 3: 14-51.

Adibe, J. (2011, September 1). "Beyond Boko Haram." Daily Trust (Abuja).

Adler, N. J. (1991). International Dimensions of Organizational Behavior. Boston, MA: PWS-Kent.

Afegbua, S. I. & Adejuwon, K. D. (2012). The Challenges of Leadership and Governance in Africa. International Journal of Academic Research in Business and Social Sciences, 2(9): 141-157.

Ake, C. (1993). The unique case of African democracy. International Affairs, 69(2): 239-244.

Ake, C. (1996). Democracy and Development in Africa. Washington, D.C.: The Brookings Institution.

Ake, C. (2001). Democracy and Development in Africa. Washington, DC: Brookings Institution.

Akindele, R. A. (1988). The Organization of African Unity, 1963-1998, Ibadan: Vintage Press.

Alibert, J. (1996). "Un bilan de la devaluation du franc CFA." Afrique Contemporaine, No. 179.

Allio, R.J. (2013). Leaders and Leadership - main theories, but what advice is reliable? Strategy and Leadership 41(1): 4-14.

Amin, S. (1977). Imperialism and Unequal Development. New York and London: Monthly Review Press.

Amin, S. (2011). Global History: A View from the South. Cape Town, Dakar, Nairobi and Oxford: Pambazuka Press.

Amnesty International. (2010). Safer to Stay Silent: The Chilling Effect of Rwanda's Laws on 'Genocide Ideology' and 'Sectarianism' Index: AFR 47/005/2010. August 2010. London: Amnesty International.

Anastasia, S. (2005). The Rwanda Conflict: Origin, Development, Exit Strategies. A Study ordered by The National Unity and Reconciliation Commission.

Anderson, B. (1991). Imagined Communities. London, Verso.

Annan, K. (2000). The Situation in Africa: the impact of AIDS on peace and security. New York: UN Security Council.

Antonakis, J. et al. (2004). The Nature of Leadership. Thousand Oaks, CA: Sage Publications.

Areji, A.C. (2005). Eurocentricity, Afrocentricity, and Globalization in Uche, 11: 65.

Asante, M. K. & Abarry, A. S. (1996). African Intellectual Heritage: A Book of Sources. Philadelphia, PA: Temple University Press.

Atangana, M. R. (1997). French Capitalism and Nationalism in Cameroon. African Studies Review, 40(1): 83-111.

Ayittey, G. B.N. (1991). Indigenous African Institutions. Ardsley-on-Hudson, NY: Transnational Publishers.

Ayittey, G. B.N. (1993). Africa Betrayed. New York: St. Martin's Press.

Bass, B. M. (1985). Leadership and Performance beyond Expectations. New York: The Free Press.

Bates, R. H. (1981). Markets and States in Tropical Africa: The Political Basis of Agricultural Policies. Berkeley: University of California Press.

Battle, M. (1997). Reconciliation: The Ubuntu Theology of Desmond Tutu. Cleveland, OH: Pilgrim Books.

Bayart, J. (1993). The State in Africa: The Politics of the Belly. London: Longman.

Billsberry, J. (2009). Discovering Leadership. New York: Palgrave MacMillan.

Blitz-Lexikon, M. (1932). Ethnographic Map of Africa.

Blunt, P. & Jones, M. (1997). Exploring the Limits of Western Leadership Theory in East Asia and Africa. Personnel Review, 26(1-2): 6-23.

Bolden, R. & Kirk, P. (2009). African Leadership: Surfacing New Understandings through Leadership Development. International Journal of Cross-Cultural Management, 9(1): 69-86.

Bond, P. (2006). Looting Africa: The Economics of Exploitation. London and New York: Zed Books.

Boon, M. (1996). The African Way: The Power of Interactive Leadership. Johannesburg: Zebra Press.

Bratton, M. & Van de Wallet, N. (1993). Neopatrimonial Regimes and Political Transitions in Africa. World Politics, pp. 46.

Bratton, M., & Nicolas, v. (1997). Democratic Experiments in Africa: Regime Transitions in Comparative Perspective. Cambridge: Cambridge University Press.

Bratton, M., & Rothschild, D. (1992). "The Institutional Bases of Governance in Africa," in Hyden, G. and Bratton, M. (eds.), Governance and Politics in Africa. Boulder & London: Lynne Rienner Publishers.

Brian, L. (1989). Apartheid: A History. New York: George Braziller.

Brown, M. B. (1995). Africa's Choices: After Thirty Years of the World Bank. London: Penguin.

Calderisi, R. (2006). The Trouble with Africa: Why Foreign Aid Isn't Working. New York: Palgrave Macmillan.

Carla, K. & Josh, H. (2016, February 25). Democracy in African Countries: Five Myths Explored. The Guardian (UK).

Chabal, P., & Jean-Pascal, D. (1999). Africa Works: Disorder as Political Instrument. Oxford: James Currey.

Chancellor, W. (1987). The Destruction of Black Civilization. Chicago: Third World Press.

Cheikh, A. D. (1987). Black Africa: The Economic and Cultural Basis for a Federated State. Trenton, NJ: Africa World Press.

Cheru, F. (1989). The Silent Revolution in Africa; Debt, Development, and Democracy. Harare: Anvil.

Cheru, F. (2002). African Renaissance: Roadmaps to the Challenge of Globalization. New York: Zed Books.

Christensen, J. (no date). Africa's Lost Tax Revenue: Lost Development Opportunities. Retrieved October 2020, from http://concernedafricascholars.org/bulletin/issue87/christensen/

Christie, P., Lessem, R., & Mbigi, L. (eds.) (1994). African

Management: Philosophies, Concepts, and Applications. Randburg: Knowledge Resources.

Clapham, C. (1982). Private Patronage and Pubic Power, London: Pinter.

Clapham, C. (1993). Democratization in Africa: Obstacles and Prospects. Third World Quarterly, 14(3): 425.

Clapham, C. (1996). Africa and the International System: The Politics of State Survival. Cambridge: Cambridge University Press.

Clapham, C. (2001). Rethinking African States. African Security Review, 10(3).

Clark, P. (2010). The Gacaca Courts, post-Genocide Justice and Reconciliation in Rwanda: Justice without borders. New York: Cambridge University Press.

Claude, A. (1982). Social Science as Imperialism: A Theory of Political Development. Ibadan: Ibadan University Press.

Coleman, J. S., & Carl G. R., (1970). Political parties and National Integration in Tropical Africa. Berkeley: University of California Press.

David Y. (1991). The Prize: The Epic Quest for Oil, Money, and Power. New York: Simon and Schuster.

Davidson, B. (1992). The Black man's Burden: Africans and the Curse of the Nation-state. London: James Currey.

Davidson, B. (1998). West African before the Colonial Era: A History to 1850. London: Longman.

Death, W. (2001). The Deep Blue Sea: Rethinking the Source of

Leadership. San Francisco: Jossey-Bass.

Decalo, S. (1990). Coups and Army Rule in Africa: Motivations and Constraints, New haven: Yale University Press.

Desmond, T. (1994). The Rainbow People of God: The Making of a Peaceful Revolution. New York: Double Day.

Dia, M. (1994). Indigenous Management Practices: Lessons for Africa's Management in the 90s, in Serageldin, I. & Taboroff, J. (Ed.). Culture and Development in Africa. Washington, DC: World Bank.

Dibie, R. & Dibie, J. (2017). Analysis of the Paralysis of Government Leadership in Sub-Saharan Africa. Africa's Public Service Delivery and Performance Review, 5(1): 167.

Dike, K. O. (1980). The Aro of South-Eastern Nigeria 1650-1980: A Study of Socio-Economic Formation and Transformation in Nigeria. Ibadan: University Press.

Dorman, S.R. (2006). Post-Liberation Politics in Africa: Examining the Political legacy of struggle. Third World Quarterly, 27(6): 1085-1101.

Dreher, A., & Herzfeld, T. (2005). The Economic Costs of Corruption: A Survey and New Evidence. New York: Mimeo.

Edem, K. (1987). Africa Tomorrow. New York: Continuum.

Englebert, P. (2000). State Legitimacy and Development in Africa. Boulder, CO: Lynne Rienner.

Englebert, P., & Rebecca, H. (2005). Let's stick together: understanding Africa's secessionist deficit. Journal of African Affairs, 104(416): 399-427.

Esebede, O. (1994). Pan-Africanism: The idea and Movement 1776-1991. Washington, DC: Howard University Press.

Eulau, H., & Susan, Z. (1999). Harold D. Lasswell's Legacy to Mainstream Political: A Neglected Agenda. Annual Review of Political Science, 2: 75–89.

Eyong, J. E. (2016). Indigenous African Leadership: Key differences from Anglo-centric thinking and writings. Leadership, 13(2): 134-149.

Falola, T. (1987). Britain and Nigeria: Exploitation or development? London: Zed Press.

Fanon, F. (1963). The Wretched of the Earth. (eds.) New York: Grove Press.

Fatton, R. (1992). Predatory Rule: State and Civil Society in Africa. Boulder: Lynne Rienner.

Folarin, S. (2010). Africa's Leadership Challenges in the 21st Century: A Nigerian Perspective. African Journal of Political Science and International Relations, 7(1): 1-11.

Gakou, M. (1987). The Crisis in African Agriculture. London: Zed Books.

Gault, H. C. (2006). New News out of Africa: Uncovering Africa's Renaissance. New York: Oxford University Press.

Gbenga, L. (2007). Corruption and Development in Africa: Challenges for Economic and Political Development. Humanity and Social Sciences Journal, 2(1): 1-7.

George, A. (1999, May 3). New Light on the Dark Continent. The

Guardian (London), Media section, 4-5.

George, P. (1963). History of the Pan-African Congress: Colonial Colored Unity, A Programme of Action. London: Panaf.

Gilbert, M. K. (1994). Allies in Adversity: The Frontline States in Southern African Security 1975-1993. Athens: Ohio University Press.

Global Trade Statistics 2019. (n.d.). Trade Statistics for Selected Countries. Comtrade. Retrieved from https://comtrade.un.org/

Godwin, A. J. (1957). The Medieval Empire of Ghana. South African Archeological Society, 12(47): 108-112.

Goran, H. (2006). African Politics in Comparative Perspective. Cambridge: Cambridge University Press.

Graig, E. J. (2005). Meeting the Ethical Challenges of Leadership. New Delhi: Sage Publications.

Griffiths, L. L. (1995). The African Inheritance. London: Routledge.

Grint, K. (2005). Leadership: Limits and Possibilities. New York: Palgrave Macmillan.

Gullestrup, H. (2006). Cultural Analysis: Towards Cross-cultural Understanding. Aalborg: Aalborg University Press.

Gusfavson, C. G. (1955). A Preface to History. New York: McGraw-Hill.

Haag, D. (2011). Mechanisms of Neocolonialism: Current French and British Influence in Cameroon and Ghana. ICIP Working Papers: 2011/6.

Hagen, E. (1962). On the Theory of Social Change: How Economic

Growth Begins. Homewood, IL: Dorsey Press.

Harsch, E. (2013). The Legacies of Thomas Sankara: A Revolutionary Experience in Retrospect. Review of African Political Economy, 40(137).

Harvey, R. (2001). The Fall of Apartheid: The Inside Story from Smut to Mbeki. New York: Palgrave Macmillan.

Henry, S. W. (1977). The Imperial Experience in Sub-Saharan Africa since 1870. Minneapolis, MN: University of Minneapolis Press.

Hill, R. A. (1987). Pan-African Biography. Los Angeles, CA: Crossroads Press.

Hobsbawn, E. J., & Terence, O. R. (1992). The Invention of Tradition. Cambridge: Cambridge University Press.

Hofstede, G. (1980). Culture's Consequences: International Differences in Work-related Values. Beverly Hills, CA: Sage Publications.

Hofstede, G. (2001). Culture's Consequences: Comparing Values, Behaviors, Institutions, and Organizations across Nations. Thousand Oaks, CA: Sage Publications.

Hofstede, G. (2011). Dimentionalizing Cultures: The Hofstede Model in Context. Online Readings in Psychology and Culture, 2(1).

Hussain, I. & Rashid, F. (1994). Adjustment in Africa; Lessons from Country Case Studies. Washington: World Bank.

Ihonvbere, J. O. (2000). Africa and the New World Order. New York: Peter Lang Publishing, Inc.

Ike, O., & Oronto, D. (2001). Where Vultures Feast: 40 Years of Shell in the Niger Delta, San Francisco, CA: Sierra Club Books.

Iliffe, J. (1995). Africans: The History of a Continent. Cambridge University Press.

Jackson, R. H., & Carl, G. R. (1982). Personal Rule in Black Africa: Prince, Autocrat Prophet, Tyrant. Berkeley: University of California Press.

Jallow, B. G. (ed.) (2013). Leadership in Colonial Africa: Disruption of Traditional Frameworks and Patterns. New York: Palgrave Macmillan.

Jallow, B. G. (eds.) (2014). Leadership in Post-colonial Africa: Trends Transformed by Independence. New York: Palgrave Macmillan.

James, D. (1961). Portuguese Africa. Cambridge, MA: Harvard University Press.

Japhace, P. & Edward, S. M. (2015). Africa's Leadership Challenges in the 21st Century: What Can Leaders Learn from Africa's Pre-colonial Leadership and Governance? International Journal of Social Science Studies.

Java, P. S. (2001). Do We Really 'Know' and 'Profess'? Decolonizing Management Knowledge. Organizational, 8(2): 227-233.

Jaycox, E. (1992). The Challenges of African Development. Washington: World Bank.

Jeremy, H. (1993). Small Wars, Small Mercies: Journeys in Africa's Disputed Nations. London: Penguin Press.

Jerven, M. (2013). Poor numbers: How we are misled by African development statistics and what to do about it. Ithaca: Cornell

University Press.

Jo-Ansie, V.W. (2007). Political Leaders in Africa: Presidents, Patrons, or Profiteers. Occasional Paper Series, 2(1).

John, M. M. (2004). NEPAD and Prospects for Development in Africa. International Studies, 41(4): 5-6.

Jones, M. L. (1986). Management Development: An African Focus. Management Education and Development, 17(3): 202-216.

Kalu, K. A. (1995). The Political Economy of Foreign Policy in ECOWAS (Book Review). Africa Today, 42: 153-156.

Kamoche, K. (1997). Managing Human Resources in Africa: Strategic Organizational and Epistemological Issues. International Business Review, 6(5): 537-555.

Kaufman, D. (1997). Corruption: The Facts. Foreign Policy, 17: 14-31.

Kew, D. (2005). Building Democracy in 21st Century Africa: Two Africas, One Solution. The Whitehead Journal of Diplomacy and International Relations, Winter/Spring: 149-161.

Khapiya, V. B. (1998) The African Experience: An Introduction. Upper Saddle River, NJ: Prentice-Hall.

Kingsley, M. H. (1897). Travels in West Africa: Congo Français, Corisco and Camerons. London: Virago.

Kodjo, E. (1987). Africa Tomorrow. London: Continuum.

Kretzschmar, L., Msiza, M., & Ntami, T. (eds.) (1997). Personality Types and Leadership Styles. Johannesburg: Baptist Convention South Africa.

Kriesberg, L. (2003). Constructive Conflict Resolution: From Escalation to Resolution. Oxford: Rowman and Littlefield.

Kuada, J. (2008). Social Resources and Entrepreneurial Activities in Africa. International Journal of Social Entrepreneurship, 1(1): 27-55.

Kuada, J. (2010). Culture and Leadership in Africa: A conceptual Model and Research Agenda. African Journal of Economic and Management Studies.

Kwame, N. (1962). Towards Colonial Freedom: Africa in the Struggle against World Imperialism. London: Heinemann

Kwame, N. (1963). Africa Must Unite. New York: International Publishers.

Lamb, D. (1984). The Africans. New York: Random House.

Landsberg, C. (2000). Promoting Democracy: The Mandela-Mbeki Doctrine. Journal of Democracy, 11(3).

Langley, J. A. (1979). Ideologies and Liberation in Black Africa, 1856-1970. London: Rex Collings.

Lederach, J. P. (1997). Building Peace: Sustainable Reconciliation in Divided Societies. Washington, DC: United States Institute of Peace Press.

Lenin, V. I. (1939). Imperialism: The Highest Stage of Capitalism. New York: International Publishers.

Lituchy, T. R. (2017). LEAD: Leadership Effectiveness in Africa and the African Diaspora. New York: Palgrave Macmillan.

Liv, J. (2012). Western Impact on Africa's Economic Development and the Progress of Democracy. Graduate Theses and Dissertations,

12872.

Louw, D. J. (1998). Ubuntu: An African Assessment of Religious Order. Twentieth World Congress of Philosophy, 23: 34-42.

Lugard, F. D. (1922). The Dual Mandate in British Tropical Africa. London: Blackwood & Sons.

Maathai, W. (2009). The Challenge for Africa. Prescott, AZ: Anchor Books.

Malunga, C. (2005). Learning Leadership Development from African Cultures: A Personal Perspective. Praxis Note No. 25.

Mamdani, M. (1996). Citizen and Subject: Contemporary Africa and the Legacy of Late Colonialism. Princeton, NJ: Princeton University Press.

Mamdani, M. (2005). "Identity and National Governance," in Wisner, B. et al. (eds.) Towards a New Map of Africa, pp. 266. London: Earthscan.

Manfred, F. R. et al. (2016). Destructive and Transformational Leadership in Africa. Africa Journal of Management.

Martin, K. (2001). Globalization and the South: Some Critical Issues. Ibadan: Spectrum Books Ltd.

Masango, M. (2002). Leadership in the African Context. Verbum et Ecclesia, 23(3).

Mazrui, A. A. (1986). The Africans: A Triple Heritage. New York: Little Brown.

Mazrui, A. A. (1995). Pan-Africanism: From Poetry to Power Issue. A Journal of Opinion, 23(1).

Mbigi, L. (1995). Ubuntu: The Spirit of African Transformation Management. Johannesburg: Knowledge Resources.

Mbigi, L. (1997). Ubuntu: The African Dream in Management. Randburg: Knowledge Resources.

Mbigi, L. (2000). In Search of the African Business Renaissance. Randburg: Knowledge Resources.

Mbigi, L. (2005). The Spirit of African Leadership. Randburg: Knowledge Resources.

Mbiti, J.S. (1997). Introduction to African Religion. London: Heinemann.

Meredith, M. (2007). The fate of Africa: A history of fifty years of independence. New York: Public Affairs.

Metz, T. (2013). The Western Ethic of Care or an Afro-communitarian Ethic? Finding the right relational morality. Journal of Global Ethics, 9: 77-92.

Metz, T. (2020). An African Theory of Good Leadership. International Journal of Ethical Leadership, 7(7).

Mills, G. (2011). Why Africa is Poor and What Africans can do about it. Johannesburg: Penguin Books.

Mintzberg, H., & Gosling, J. (2002). Educating Managers Beyond Borders. Academy of Management Learning & Education, 1(1): 64-76.

Mkapa, B (2005, August 25). African Continent Needs Home Grown Democracy. The New Humanitarian

Molefi, A. (1991, September 23). Putting Africa at the Centre.

Newsweek Magazine, pp. 42.

Molefi, K. A. (2003). Afrocentricity: A Theory of Social Change. Chicago: African American Images.

Monroe, J. C. (2013). Power and Agency in Pre-colonial African States. Annual Review of Anthropology, 42: 17-35.

Moyo, D. (2009). Dead Aid: Why Aid Is Not Working and How There Is a Better Way for Africa. London: Allen Lane.

Muchiri, M. K. (2011). Leadership in Context: A Review and Research Agenda for sub-Saharan Africa. Journal of Occupational and Organizational Psychology, 84: 440-452.

Muczyk, J. P. & Holt, D. (2008). Toward a Cultural Contingency Model of Leadership. Journal of Leadership and Organizational Studies, 14(4): 277-286.

Murithi, T. (2008). African Indigenous and Endogenous Approaches to Peace and Conflict Resolution. In Francis, D. J. (ed). Peace and Conflict in Africa. London: Zed Books.

Ndlovu, P. M. (2016). Discovering the spirit of Ubuntu leadership. London: Palgrave Macmillan.

Nelson, M. (1995). Long Walk to Freedom: The Autobiography of Nelson Mandela. Boston, MA: Little, Brown, and Company.

Nganje, F. (2015). Moving Beyond Africa's Crisis of Institutions. Governance and APRM Programme. Occasional Paper 222.

Northouse, P.G. (2004). Leadership: Theory and Practice. Thousand Oaks, CA: Sage Publications.

Ntalaja-Nzongola, G. (2005). The Congo: From Leopold to Kabila:

A People's History. New York: ZED Books.

Nwala, T. U. (1992). Critical Review of the Great Debate on African Philosophy (1970-1990). Nsukka: William Amo Centre for African Philosophy, University of Nigeria.

Nyang, S. S. (1984). Islam, Christianity, and African Identity. Brattleboro, VT: Amana Books.

Obasanjo: The lust for power and its tragic implications for Nigeria. Zaria: Vanguard Publishers.

Obiakor, F. (2004). Building Patriotic African Leadership through African-centered Education. Journal of Black Studies, 34(3): 402-420.

Obiyo, C. (2011). Should African Nations Forgive and Forget? Retrieved October 1, 2020, from http://myafricanplan.com/2011/01/should-african-nations-forgive-and-forget/

Ochola, S. A. (2007). Leadership and Economic Crisis in Africa. Nairobi: Kenya Literature Bureau.

OECD/AfDB (2006). African Economic Outlook 2006. Paris: OECD Publishing.

Okechukwu, E. A. (2019). Globalization and Leadership in Africa: Developments and Challenges for the Future. Cham: Palgrave MacMillan.

Organski, A.F.K. (1965). The Stages of Political Development. New York: Knopf Overseas Development.

Osabu-kle, D. T. (2000). Compatible Cultural Democracy: The key to

Development in Africa. Ontario: Broadview Press.

Oye, O. (1986). The International Politics of Africa's Strategic Minerals. Westport, CT: Greenwood Press.

Paul, N., & Asiwaju, A. I. (1996). African Boundaries: Barriers, Conduits, and Opportunities. London: Pinter.

Poncian, J. & Mgaya, E. S. (2015). Africa's Leadership Challenges in the 21st Century: What Can Leaders Learn from Africa's Pre-colonial Leadership and Governance? International Journal of Social Science Studies, 3(3): 105-114.

Porteous, T. (2008). Britain in Africa. London: Zed Press.

Rajani, K. K. (2009). The Challenge of Eurocentrism: Global Perspectives, Policies, and Prospects. New York: Palgrave Macmillan.

Randall, R. (2000). The Debt: What America Owes to Blacks. New York: Dutton Books.

Ray, D.I., & Reddy, P.S. (eds.) (2002). Grassroots Governance? Chiefs in Africa and the Afro-Caribbean. Calgary: University of Calgary Press.

Robert, G. (2004). The Shackled Continent. London: Macmillan Press.

Robert, J. et al. (2004). Culture, Leadership, and Organization: The Globe Study of 62 Societies. New Delhi: Sage Publications.

Roberts, J. M. (1993). A History of the World. New York: Oxford University Press.

Rodney, W. (1972). How Europe Underdeveloped Africa. London: Bogle-L'Ouverture Publications.

Rost, J.C. (1991). Leadership for the 21st Century. Westport, CT: Praeger.

Rostow, W. W. (1960). The stages of economic growth: A non-communist manifesto. Cambridge, UK: Cambridge University Press.

Rotberg, R. I. (1988). The Founder: Cecil Rhodes and the Pursuit of Power. New York: Oxford University Press.

Sandbrook, R. (1985). The Politics of Africa's Economic Stagnation, Cambridge: Cambridge University Press.

Sanford, J. U. (1985). Africa: The People and Politics of an Emerging Continent. New York: Simon Schuster.

Senghor, L. S. (1986). Afrique Nouvelle II cited in Afrocommunism by M. Ottaway & D. Ottaway. New York: Africana Publications.

Serageldin, I., & Taboroff, J. (eds.) Culture and Development in Africa. Washington university DC: World Bank.

Sindima, H. J. (1995). Africa's Agenda: The Legacy of Liberalism and Colonialism in the Crisis of African Values. Westport: Greenwood.

Sklar, R. L. (1979). The Nature of Class Domination in Africa. Journal of Modern African Studies, 7(14): 531-52

Southall, R., & Melber, H. (eds.) (2006). Legacies of Power: Leadership, Change and Former Presidents in African Politics. Cape Town: HSRC Press.

Stogdill, R. M. (1974). Handbook of Leadership: A Survey of Theory and Research. New York: The Free Press.

Sutton, F. X. et al. (1989). Development Ideology: Its Emergence and Decline. Daedalus, 118(1): 35-60.

Tangwa, G. (1998). Democracy and Development in Africa: Putting the Horse Before the Cart. Road Companion to Democracy and Meritocracy. Bellington, WA: Kola Tree Resources.

The Economist (2016). Democracy Index 2016: Revenge of the "deplorables." The Economist Intelligence Unit.

The Guardian. (1994, August 12). Nigeria Loses Clout to South Africa. Lagos: The Guardian Newspapers.

Thiam, T. (2003). Political Leadership and the Quest for Unity and Development in Africa. Master's Thesis: Eastern Illinois University.

Thomas, P. (1991). The Scramble for Africa: White Man's Conquest of the Dark Continent from 1876 to 1912. New York: Avon Books.

Thomson, A. (2000). An Introduction to African Politics. London: Routledge.

Tlou, T., & Campbell, A. (1984). History of Botswana. Gaborone and Basingstoke: Macmillan.

Tutu, D. (1999). No Future without Forgiveness. London: Rider Random House.

Twowo, V. A. (2011). Knowing in Context: A Post-colonial Analysis of Contemporary Leadership Development. Ph. D. Thesis. Exeter University.

Van der Colff, L. (2002a). Leadership Lessons from the African Tree: Multicultural Business Issues and Practices. International Academy of African Business and Development.

Van der Colff, L. (2002b). Ubuntu, isivivane and uhluhlasa: The Meaning of Leadership and Management in Developing Philosophy of Management in South Africa. Oxford: St Anne's College.

Wambu, O. (ed.) (2007). Under the Tree of Talking: Leadership for Change in Africa. London: Counterpoint.

Warren, B. (1980). Imperialism: The Pioneer of Capitalism. London: Verso.

William, R. (1998). Warlord Politics and African States. Boulder, CO: Lynne Rienner.

Wiseman, J. A. (1995). Democracy and Political Change in Sub-Saharan Africa, London: Routledge.

Wolf, M. (2016). Democrats, demagogues, and despots. London: Financial Times.

World Bank (1994). Adjustment in Africa: Reforms, Results, and the Road Ahead. New York: Oxford University Press.

World Bank. (1997). Taking Action to Reduce Poverty in sub-Saharan Africa. Washington, DC: World Bank Publications.

World Bank. (1997). World Development Report 1997. New York: Oxford University Press.

Young, C. (1994). The African Colonial State in Comparative Perspective. New Haven, CT: Yale University Press.

Index

Q

R

S

widespread, 81, 102, 103, 118, 152, 160, 194
wield, 23, 59
wielded, 82
William du Bois, 38
willingness, 128, 139, 147, 192
Winston Churchill, 50
Wolof, 59
women, 32, 33, 43, 44, 45, 46, 142, 148, 175, 202, 228, 289
Work Ethics, 254
World Bank, 53, 239, 251, 267, 269, 272, 273, 281, 283
World Trade Organization, 33, 197
worldview, 31, 132, 193, 203, 238, 254
worrisome, 180
WWI, 89, 110, 124, 165, 222

X
Xhosa people, 102

Y
Yang, 237
Yin, 237
Yoruba, 26, 65, 71, 72

Z
Zambia, 51, 76, 103, 114, 115, 119, 120, 128
Zanzibar Revolution, 99
Zaria, 44, 279
zeal, 90
Zimbabwe, 22, 23, 24, 25, 28, 30, 51, 66, 67, 83, 103, 114, 115, 119, 120, 128, 155, 156
Zimbabwe African National, 156
Zimbabwe African National Union-Patriotic Front (ZANU-PF), 156

**STEPHENS
LEADERSHIP
CONSULTANCY**

We are a team of experts bringing our knowledge and many years of experience, offering new insights into your business and knowledge about what you could be doing better.

We also help to set clearer plans, improve workforce morale and productivity, and develop business strategies that aim at meeting company's long-term goals. Find below our areas of expertise:

- Management Consulting
- Research and Analytics
- Regulatory Compliance
- Leadership Coaching

- Business Analysis
- Foresight and Innovation Strategy
- Executive Capacity Optimisation
- Human Capital Development

- Project Management
- Corporate Governance
- Organizational Architecture
- Culture Change

@stephensleader
@stephensleadership
Stephens Leadership Consultancy
Stephens Leadership Consultancy

+1267 339 8385
+234 708 802 5591
www.stephensleadership.com
contactus@stephensleadership.com

Texas, United States
Stephens Leadership Consultancy LLC
110 W Randol Mill Rd, Suite 240 Arlington, TX 76011

Lagos, Nigeria
Stephens Leadership Consultancy Limited
19, Oladipo Bateye St. GRA Ikeja, Lagos

The
Leadership
Factory

The Leadership Factory *With* Toye Sobande

Exceptional leadership by ordinary people

Every Sunday Evening

8pm - Nigeria (GMT +1)
2pm - USA (CST)
8pm - UK (GMT)
3pm - Canada (EST)

@toyesobande

Linked in
@Emmanuel Toye Sobande

About the Book

Africa is a continent rich in human and material resources yet perceived to be bereft of leaders imbued with requisite leadership skills to harness these resources for her growth and development. There are plausible reasons why universally acclaimed leadership principles do not work in Sub-Saharan Africa. This book posits that these leadership principles were Eurocentric principles forced down the throat of Africans by their heavy-handed and exploitative colonial masters who cared less about the sociology and anthropology of the peoples of Africa, and their governance structures, which hitherto worked for them in their different locales and settlements.

It argues that pre-colonial Africa was not utterly primitive, lacking leaders nor bereft of leadership principles as painted by the European colonialists who were everything but altruistic in their dealings with the peoples of Sub-Saharan Africa. To buttress this point, it paints a rich canvass of several defunct kingdoms across Sub-Saharan Africa whose leaders exhibited excellent leadership skills and organisational prowess that ensured order and stability in and within their domains. Painfully, the fall or decimation of these kingdoms cannot be delinked from the partitioning of Africa by the Europeans at the Berlin Conference. Indeed, the fall of Africa began at the Berlin Conference.

To solve Africa's leadership challenge, today's leaders of Africa must study the pre-colonial leaders of Africa and the leadership skills they exhibited, which engendered cohesion, order, peace, and development in their domains, and by so doing adopt those leadership principles that are centred on the norms, mores, cultures, and traditions of African peoples, known as "Afrocentrism." The book goes further to list out the benefits derivable from adopting the concept of Afrocentrism if Africa wants to regain its lost glory while stressing that Eurocentric leadership will never work in Africa because Afrocentric leadership principles are tightly hinged on the ubuntu or omoluwabi principle, which places a huge emphasis on communalism, collectivity, and unity of purpose, as well as on empathy for others unlike the Eurocentric leadership principle, which is straitjacketed, individualistic and devoid of empathy.

Africa is not as bereft of quality leaders as painted by European colonialists and neocolonialists; the book extolls the leadership, managerial and organisational skills of notable and globally acclaimed leaders such as South Africa's, Nelson Mandela, Nigeria's Ngozi Okonjo-Iweala, Akinwunmi Adesina also of Nigeria, and a host of other Africans who has shown that Africa does not lack the people, but even in this 21st Century; parades men and women who have and still holds their own on the world stage across professions and human endeavours.

This book is a must-read for academics/scholars, students, politicians, administrators, and if you are not any of those, you are still asked to get a copy. It will open your minds and eyes to Africa's great potential if she finds solutions to her leadership challenge.

Other Books by Toye Sobande

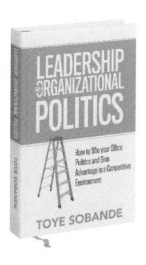

**Leadership and
Organizational Politics :**
How to Win your Office
Politics and Gain
Advantage in a
Competitive Environment

The Leadership Factory :
Human Resource
Development Practices
That Helps Organizations
And Businesses Define,
Develop And Deploy
Leadership Capabilities

Made in the USA
Coppell, TX
07 January 2022